101 Ways to Cut Your Business Insurance Costs without Sacrificing Protection

William S. McIntyre IV

Jack P. Gibson

McGraw-Hill Book Company
New York   St. Louis   San Francisco   Auckland
Bogotá   Hamburg   London   Madrid   Mexico
Milan   Montreal   New Delhi   Panama
Paris   São Paulo   Singapore
Sydney   Tokyo   Toronto

McIntyre, William Stokes.
  101 ways to cut your business insurance costs
without sacrificing protection.

  Includes index.
  1. Insurance, Business, 2. Insurance, Business—
United States. I. Gibson, Jack P. II. Title.
III. Title: One hundred one ways to cut your business
insurance costs without sacrificing protection.
HG8059.M38 1988 368   87-17255
ISBN 0-07-045112-5

This book includes, with permission, material from the following
International Risk Management Institute, Inc.,
publications: *Construction Risk Management, Risk Financing, Commercial
Liability Insurance* and *Glossary of Insurance and Risk Management
Terms.* Also included is copyright material of the National Council
on Compensation Insurance, used with permission.

1234567890   DOCDOC   89210987

ISBN 0-07-045112-5

The editors for this book were Martha Jewett and Esther Gelatt, the
designer was Naomi Auerbach, and the production supervisor was
Dianne Walber. It was set in Baskerville by the McGraw-Hill Book
Company Professional and Reference Book Division composition
unit.

Printed and bound by R. R. Donnelley & Sons.

Contents

Preface

Do you think your organization pays too much for insurance? If you are like most business managers, you answered that question with a resounding "Yes!" You may also feel that you are totally at the mercy of your insurance company because you just don't understand insurance jargon, complicated policies, coverages and exclusions, and how premiums are determined. To many managers, insurance is a mysterious but necessary evil.

This does not have to be the case. You probably manage your tax liabilities on a proactive basis in order to control your tax burden as best you can. If you take the same approach with your insurance program, you can also control your insurance premiums!

However, there is one major stumbling block—not usually faced by tax managers—to taking control of property and liability insurance costs. While the Internal Revenue Code is a published document in the public domain, the insurance industry's "rating manuals," which govern how your premiums are calculated, are not easily obtainable. And, like the tax laws, you would probably need an interpreter to explain how to apply them to your business, were you able to locate these rating manuals at all.

101 Ways to Cut Your Business Insurance Costs does this for you. As your personal insurance interpreter, it summarizes and explains how your premiums are calculated. More important, it tells you about the "tricks of the trade" used to calculate your organization's premiums. Knowledge of these approaches and of the important "risk management" techniques reviewed in this book can save your business hundreds or even thousands of premium dollars. This book is based on our experience over the years as consultants for numerous commercial and public entities, as insurance agents on behalf of commercial insureds, and as researchers into insurance industry practices and procedures. We have attempted to explain in plain English how you can reduce or control your business insurance costs without exposing your organization to uninsured losses that it cannot handle. If your business, public, or nonprofit organization can benefit from just a few of these ideas, our efforts will have been worthwhile.

William S. McIntyre IV
Jack P. Gibson

101 Ways to Cut Your Business Insurance Costs without Sacrificing Protection

1
Introduction

Insurance, particularly in recent times, has become a major cost item to American business. For most business people, the method by which the insurance industry determines the premiums it will charge for property and liability insurance is a complete mystery. Thus, *101 Ways to Cut Your Business Insurance Costs* has been prepared to shed some light on the insurance industry's approach to pricing its product and to alert business managers to ways of controlling their organizations' property and casualty insurance costs.

Insurance Premium Determination

The premium for an insurance policy is calculated by determining a *rate* which is then applied to some measurement of the business's propensity to have losses or claims (called the *exposure base*). For many types of insurance, the rate is found by simply looking it up in a manual published by an insurance industry rating bureau. While members of the public can obtain these rating manuals much more easily than in the past, they are not available in bookstores across the nation. Depending upon the type of insurance, the rates applicable to a particular organization will vary in accordance with geographic location (some regions have more automobiles on the road, poorer fire departments, or a more litigious social environment), the type of property or operation being insured (wood frame buildings cost more to insure than masonry structures), protective safeguards in place (it costs less to insure a building with a sprinkler system than one that has none), and other similar types of variables. The rating manuals which contain these rates are prepared by insurance company associations, called *rating bureaus*.

Rating Bureaus

Typically, rating bureaus are nonprofit organizations which serve their member insurance companies. They collect statistical data for these insurance companies and use this data to determine recommended insurance rates. They then file these rates on behalf of their member insurance companies with state insurance regulators. Sometimes, insurance companies use these rates verbatim, but they may also deviate from them.

The most important insurance industry rating bureaus are probably the National Council on Compensation Insurance (NCCI), the Insurance Services Office (ISO), and the Surety Association of America (SAA). The NCCI collects statistical data, provides rating information, and promulgates "standard" policy forms for workers compensation insurance. It currently has over 700 members. ISO provides virtually the same types of services for nearly every line of insurance with the exception of workers compensation insurance, surety bonds, fidelity bonds, excess/umbrella liability, and certain lines of professional liability insurance. In other words, ISO provides insurers with rating data and promulgates standard policy forms for such lines of insurance as commercial property, commercial automobile, commercial crime, boiler and machinery, inland marine, and commercial general liability. ISO currently has approximately 1,300 participating companies in the United States. The SAA provides rating information and promulgates standard policy forms for fidelity insurance (e.g., commercial crime policies, public official bonds, financial institution bonds, etc.) and surety bonds (e.g., performance and payment and bonds).

Proactive Approach to Insurance Purchasing

While the insurance rating process sounds and really is simple, there is much more to it than simply looking up a "manual rate" in a book and multiplying it by an exposure base. There are published "rules" in the insurance industry's rating manuals which guide the insurance underwriters and rate technicians in determining the exposure base to use, in choosing the most appropriate rate from the manual, and in deviating from published rates. If insurance buyers knew all of these rules, they would know what actions to take to ensure that the rate chosen for the business was the lowest one possible. In addition, areas where mistakes could be made by the insurance companies in determining and calculating premiums would be obvious, and the business manager would be in a position to know that those mistakes did not occur when the premiums for the business's policy were determined.

This book supplies this knowledge. It provides a list of actions that the business manager can take to ensure that the lowest possible insurance rates are used in pricing the business's policies. Included are areas where the insurance industry frequently makes mistakes in calculating business insurance premiums so that the business manager can verify that these mistakes are not being made or correct them if they are. Finally, the book also points out areas in which business managers frequently make mistakes that cost them money. For too many years, commercial businesses have allowed insurance companies to calculate their premium costs with virtually no audit function in place to show that these costs were properly determined. This approach is very similar to asking the Internal Revenue Service to determine your tax liability without your input or even your understanding of how income taxation is derived. While this approach may be acceptable in "soft" insurance markets such as the one experienced from 1979 to 1984, because of competitive pressures on insurance companies, it is a costly way of doing business when the insurance market is "tight." Business managers who proactively manage their insurance programs and practice the art and science of *risk management* will be assured that their organizations are paying no more than they should for their property and casualty insurance. As a result, the competitive position of their businesses will be enhanced.

What Is Risk Management?

Risk management is nothing more than a commonsense approach to handling the potential ways in which an organization could suffer losses other than those solely attributable to business operations. In other words, risk management is an approach to protecting an organization from losses caused by fire, theft, flood, earthquake, liability lawsuits, work-related injuries to employees, and similar events. It attempts to effectively handle these "loss exposures" or "risks" at the lowest possible cost to the organization.

The process involves logical steps that anyone can follow to manage risks:

- Identify risks.
- Analyze risks.
- Select the best methods for handling the risks.

- Implement the chosen alternatives.
- Monitor the results.

Risk Identification

Identification of risks is the most important step in the process because risks that are not identified may not be contemplated in the risk management program. The result of this may be a large, unexpected, and uninsured loss. Risk identification is accomplished by carefully reviewing the organization's operations and assets to determine the ways that losses may occur. These identified risks are then analyzed in an attempt to determine the magnitude of the losses if they did occur and the potential effects on the organization. The business manager's insurance agent or broker should take an active part in this process but cannot do it without help and cooperation.

Risk Management Techniques

Once these loss exposures are identified and their potential effects on the organization are analyzed, a determination is made of which risk management techniques will best handle each loss exposure. The various risk management techniques seek to keep losses from occurring, reduce the effects of those that do occur, and/or finance the cost of losses. The most commonly used risk management techniques are:

- Avoidance
- Loss control
- Retention
- Contractual transfer
- Insurance transfer

Risk Avoidance

Avoidance involves not engaging in operations that may lead to unacceptable losses. For example, many contractors decided not to enter into the pollution cleanup business because of the high potential for catastrophic, uninsurable liability losses. Similarly, pharmaceutical companies have discontinued production of certain drugs because of the liability suits associated with occasional side effects.

Loss Control

Loss control involves reducing the potential for losses to occur and/or the effects of those that do occur. For example, the use of protective eyeglasses by workers in a manufacturing plant reduces the possibility that eye injuries to employees will occur. The installation of a building sprinkler system, on the other hand, reduces the amount of damage from a fire that does start.

Risk Retention

Retention involves the organization's paying for all or part of the losses it suffers out of operating income or, in some cases, out of a dedicated fund rather than transferring them to another party, such as an insurer. This can be achieved by taking deductibles, using rating plans that provide premium returns when losses are lower than expected or surcharges when they are higher, or by simply not buying insurance. Retention is almost always less expensive than insurance *in the long run*. In the short run, however, large retentions can cause severe budgeting and cash flow problems.

Three rules of thumb are often considered when a retention level is being selected:

1. Don't risk a great deal (of loss) for a little (premium savings).
2. Consider the odds (of a large loss or many small ones occurring).
3. Don't risk more than the organization can afford to lose.

These three rules, when followed, will generally cause the organization to retain losses that happen frequently and/or do not potentially involve large dollar amounts. These types of losses are budgetable and do not impair the financial viability of the organization when they occur. Risks that present the possibility of large, catastrophic losses should almost always be insured.

Contractual Risk Transfer

Contractual risk transfer (sometimes called *noninsurance risk transfer*) involves passing the organization's risks to others by use of hold harmless or indemnity clauses and insurance requirements in business contracts, such as leases. A hold harmless clause requires one party to hold the other party harmless for losses to a member of the public arising from operations covered by the contract. For example, a lease may require the tenant to hold the landlord harmless for lawsuits brought against the landlord by members of the public injured in the part of the premises rented to the tenant. Businesses may be able to pass some of their risks on to others in this way to reduce the need for or cost of liability insurance. They must also review contracts entered into with other parties to determine (1) what risks the other party is attempting to pass to the business and (2) how the business will handle these risks if it accepts them.

Insurance

For those risks not handled by the previous techniques, insurance is purchased. This involves the financing of the organization's losses by an insurance company. For all but the smallest organizations, insurance is an income-smoothing device that spreads the financial consequences of losses out over a period of time. The erratic, unbudgetable losses are traded for a budgetable insurance premium. However, all but the very smallest commercial insureds will, over time, reimburse their insurers for most, if not all, losses they pay on these insureds' behalf, plus a factor to cover the insurers' expenses and profits. As a general rule of thumb, 60 percent of insurance premiums is used to pay losses, with the remainder applied to overhead and profits. This fact justifies expending time and effort using the previously mentioned risk management techniques even if they do not eliminate the need for insurance. Reducing your insured losses will reduce your insurance premiums.

Monitoring the Results

Once the alternatives are chosen and implemented, it is necessary to monitor the results. It must be remembered that changes in the organization, society, and insurance marketplace will affect the continued appropriateness of past decisions. The organization's risk management program should be periodically fine-tuned as these changes occur.

Summary

In summary, risk management is a practical process for handling an organization's risks of loss other than business risks. The primary goal of the process is to ensure that the organization's income stream and/or assets are not impaired by a loss or losses to an extent that threatens the organization's survival. The second goal of risk management is to employ the least expensive risk management techniques possible to meet the primary goal. The risk management process can be applied by business managers who have insurance purchasing as one of many responsibilities or by professional, full-time risk managers. Using the process, by contemplating possible losses and taking cost-effective steps to handle them before they occur, will save the organization substantial amounts of money.

How to Use This Book

This book is divided into chapters that correspond to the various lines of insurance purchased by most businesses. It also includes chapters on some risk management topics which can lead to cost savings. The various ways of reducing or controlling business insurance costs are numbered sequentially throughout these chapters. Not all of the 101 ways will be applicable to any particular organization, and some of them are mutually exclusive. It is suggested that you first scan this book to develop a feel for its contents. Then read the related insurance coverage chapter(s) approximately 90 to 120 days prior to renewing a particular insurance policy. This will allow time for applying the various techniques prior to the policy's renewal. The chapters on agent/company relationships, claims, competitive bidding, risk financing, and the general recommendations can be applied at any time.

Also note that each chapter presents an overview of the subjects it covers before discussing ways to reduce or control costs. This is to provide background information on some important aspects of the topic. For example, the chapters dealing with specific insurance policies provide brief descriptions of their scope and application. Those chapters dealing with risk management techniques, claims, and industry relationships provide background information on the importance of claims, the insurance distribution system, or the risk management concept. These discussions should be particularly informative for readers who have not had extensive experience with insurance.

In summary, read the book as you would read any other book and then use it as, in essence, a reference to cost control. Prior to renewing any particular type of insurance policy, review the chapter related to that policy. For assistance in scanning the book, Figure 1.1 gives you a checklist of the cost-reduction ways that are discussed.

Figure 1.1. The 101 ways to cut costs.

The following is a list of the 101 ways to control business insurance costs that are discussed in this book. The various headings correspond with the titles of chapters in the book.

<u>Automobile Insurance (Chapter 2)</u>

 1. Determine proper "use" classifications.
 2. Check territories and states.
 3. Avoid distance surcharges.
 4. Watch weight classifications.
 5. Avoid premiums on mobile equipment.
 6. Use contractors' equipment floater policies.
 7. Recognize "on-premises" and industrial vehicles.
 8. Get personal vehicle rating credits.
 9. Reduce recreational vehicle premiums.
10. Consider fire, theft, and specified causes-of-loss coverage.
11. Use deductibles.
12. Self-insure collision.
13. Obtain scheduled credits/debits and dividends.
14. Use experience rating.
15. Use the suspension of insurance endorsement.
16. Understand the "stated amount" approach.
17. Discontinue medical payments and personal injury protection.
18. Drop uninsured motorists coverage where possible.
19. Think twice about rental car collision waivers.
20. Self-insure auto liability.

<u>Commercial General Liability Insurance (Chapter 3)</u>

21. Use proper classifications.
22. Use lessor's risk only classification.
23. Delete truck drivers' and pilots' payrolls.
24. Delete clerical office employees' payrolls.
25. Delete overtime surcharges.
26. Use executive officer payroll limitation.
27. Look twice at intercompany sales.
28. Delete sales taxes and excise taxes.
29. Take advantage of the transition program.
30. Use experience rating.
31. Obtain schedule credits/dividends.
32. Use deductibles.
33. Negotiate advisory (A) rates.
34. Negotiate premium credits for coverage limitations.

---

35. Drop medical payments coverage.
36. Think twice about the claims-made option.
37. Obtain certificates from contractors.

Umbrella Liability Insurance (Chapter 4)

38. Consider alternative primary limits.
39. Obtain quotes for buffer layers.
40. Get competitive pricing.
41. Submit well-prepared specifications.
42. Determine the premium basis.
43. Select reasonable umbrella limits.
44. Provide for automatic extensions.
45. Use care with adjustable rate policies.

Workers Compensation (Chapter 5)

46. Get correct classifications.
47. Delete overtime payroll surcharges.
48. Use a "first-aid folder."
49. Take advantage of dividends and flexible rates.

Experience Rating (Chapter 6)

50. Review reserves.
51. Prepare a test modifier.
52. Review final modifier.
53. Check payroll and losses used.
54. Understand acquisition, merger, and spin-off implications.
55. Correct calculation errors.

Property Insurance (Chapter 7)

56. Obtain rate deviations/dividends.
57. Use deductibles.
58. Invest in fire prevention.
59. Use business-interruption reporting form.
60. Store volatiles safely.
61. Buy Underwriters Laboratory-approved UL-90 roof.
62. Use fireproof cabinets.
63. Get duplicate records credit.
64. Obtain coinsurance credits.
65. Use reporting policies.
66. Report proper builders risk values.

Insurance Industry Relationships (Chapter 8)

67. Choose a knowledgeable agent or broker.

(*Continued*)

Figure 1.1. The 101 ways to cut costs.

68. Use a limited number of agencies/brokerages.
69. Use a written scope of engagement.
70. Maintain communication.
71. Know your underwriter.
72. Negotiate fees/commissions.
73. Use consultants.

Claims (Chapter 9)

74. Request advance payment of property claims.
75. Use public adjusters on large property losses.
76. Have periodic meetings with insurance company adjusters.
77. Obtain right to approve workers compensation and liability claims.
78. Audit claims departments.
79. Maintain loss records.

Risk Financing (Chapter 10)

80. Carefully select retrospective minimum and maximum factors.
81. Negotiate agent's commission outside rating plan.
82. Negotiate other retrospective rating factors.
83. Explore a "paid loss" retrospective rating plan.
84. Consider other cash flow programs.
85. Examine self-insurance/captive option.
86. Consider group self-insurance/captives.

Insurance Bidding (Chapter 11)

87. Don't bid too frequently.
88. Allocate insurers to the agents/brokers.
89. Allow adequate time to secure proposals.
90. Provide adequate information.
91. Don't bid "excess and surplus lines" coverages among agents.

General Recommendations (Chapter 12)

92. Consolidate effective dates.
93. Maximize purchasing power with one insurer.
94. Buy package policies.
95. Prepare or verify premium audits.
96. Defer premiums.
97. Develop a comprehensive data base.
98. Prepare early for renewals.
99. Hire a risk manager.
100. Implement contractual transfer programs.
101. Control your losses.

2
Automobile Insurance

Automobile insurance provides two types of protection, insurance for: (1) liability for injuries to others and/or damage to their property ("bodily injury liability and property damage liability") and (2) damage to owned vehicles. The liability coverage is generally referred to as *automobile liability insurance*, while damage to owned vehicles is referred to as *automobile physical damage*. In most states, coverage is provided under a policy that is referred to as the *business auto policy* (BAP), while a few states still use the older *comprehensive auto liability* (CAL) form. Automobile dealerships, parking garages, and certain equipment dealerships use the garage or dealers policies.

Besides covering exposures associated with owned vehicles, liability insurance usually covers operation of nonowned vehicles in cases such as when an employee uses a personal car to run an errand or when hired vehicles come with drivers provided by common carriers or other truckers.

There are two basic types of physical damage coverage usually provided for owned autos: collision and comprehensive. The *collision coverage* insures against damage from collision with another vehicle or object as well as from overturning. The *comprehensive coverage* provides protection against damage from other types of peril such as hail, fire, vandalism, and flood.

Before 1960, many insurance companies issued a separate policy for each and every vehicle owned by the insured. With the introduction of the comprehensive auto liability policy, coverage was afforded automatically with respect to liability for all owned vehicles and, subject to certain conditions, for auto physical damage. While some insureds report fleet additions and deletions during the year, the preferred approach is to report all fleet changes at the end of the year with the insurance company making the necessary premium adjustment at that time. This saves substantial administrative costs on the part of the business manager, insurance agent, and insurance company.

Ways to Reduce Costs

This chapter shows 20 ways to reduce automobile insurance costs.

1. Determine Proper "Use" Classifications

Taking all variables into account, there can be as many as 1,500 different premiums developed in a particular state for a commercial vehicle based on its use, weight, and garaging location and on the distance it is normally driven. This sounds like an unbelievable maze of calculations, but the process is quite logical. A manual outlining all the rating approaches is published by Insurance Services Office, Inc. (ISO). Although an insurance buyer will probably not want to purchase the manual, the insurance agent or underwriter has access to it so the buyer can review a copy.

Use Classifications. The first step in developing the premium for a commercial vehicle is to determine its "use" classification:

1. Service use
2. Retail use
3. Commercial use

   Service Use. This classification refers to the transportation of employees or property to and from job locations. Generally, it applies to contractors and those service firms that perform work off premises.

   Retail Use. This classification involves the pickup of property from a store and delivery to nonowned premises such as a residence—usually by vans or trucks.

   Commercial Use. This classification covers any use other than service or retail use. The service use classification is usually subject to the lowest rate, while vehicles falling into the commercial use classification are subject to the highest rate.

Proper Information. It is important that the insurance buyer review the actual usage of vehicles to determine if the organization's vehicles can be rated in a lower classification. Unless the buyer provides proper information, insurance underwriters tend to apply the old adage, "When in doubt, use a higher rate." As with all rules and regulations, there are many gray areas. During times of restrictive insurance markets, insurance companies tend to use the higher classifications.

Picture File. Another important technique in determining the proper classification of vehicles, especially those dispersed over a large geographical area, is to photograph the vehicles and build a file that includes the pictures, license receipts, and invoices. This enables the insurance representative to classify the vehicles more accurately and to provide a record of the actual property insured.

2. Check Territories and States

The insurance industry develops loss statistics for each state and even breaks each state into rating territories. For instance, Texas—being one of the larger states—has more than 40 territories. The reason for these territorial classifications is that experience in densely populated areas differs from that in less populated areas. Areas with high population density tend to have more accidents, due to traffic congestion, than do less dense areas. In other words, more cars produce more wrecks.

People in urban areas are more prone to litigate. They tend to sue more, sue longer, and sue for more money. This increases claims and legal costs in areas of high population. Many insureds use these territorial rating classifications to their advantage.

If vehicles are used and garaged in rural areas where rates are low, the insured who reports them as being garaged in those rural areas—rather than in the urban area where the home office is located—gains an advantage by avoiding the higher urban rates. A question arises, "Does the policy have to be revised every time there is a change in a vehicle's location?" The answer is, "No." Instead, review the automobile schedule at each policy anniversary date to determine changes in the location of vehicles and report accordingly.

Rates differ substantially from state to state. For example, average rates are higher in New York than in Texas. By planning to as great a degree as possible where automobiles will be garaged, and by being sensitive to variations in rates from territory to territory and state to state, you can substantially reduce the premiums for business automobiles.

3. Avoid Distance Surcharges

Since longer driving distances increase the possibility of accidents, insurers consider driving distances in rating auto insurance. Distance surcharges—based on the number of miles driven to and from a particular location—usually apply. The first surcharge usually applies at distances over 50 miles. A second, higher, surcharge generally applies to vehicles driven over 200 miles.

The theory is that the more miles the vehicle travels, the greater the chance of loss. Therefore, the insurance company should get additional premiums based on the longer distances driven. However, there are some questions as to how these surcharges are applied. For example, the surcharges are not to be applied until a vehicle exceeds the specified distance on a regular and frequent basis. The Illinois States Supreme Court once ruled that the term "regular and frequent" may mean 26 times a year between the same two points over that certain distance. Some insurance companies deem regular and frequent use to be once a month. As a result, there is a great deal of discussion and latitude in this area.

Also, the distance does not have to be measured in road miles but can be "as the crow flies," or the straight-line distance between two points. A location that is 60 miles away by road may be only 50 air miles away and, therefore, not subject to a surcharge.

To avoid overcharges, the insured must ask, "What distance surcharges are being applied? Are these charges really valid?" In this somewhat gray area, underwriters will be more liberal in times of a soft market. In a tight market, however, underwriters looking for any basis to increase premiums will be less willing to negotiate on this point.

While the territory classification will usually not affect the applicability of coverage, some companies add a limitation of use endorsement, suspending coverage outside a given radius. Therefore, the insured must ask whether any territorial limitation in the policy affects the coverage. If the insurance company does add a limitation of use endorsement, coverage may be severely impaired. In the past, courts have voided these limitation of use endorsements. Consequently, most insurance companies will not attach them to their policies; but some still use them.

When faced with the question of whether to have vehicles designated local with the limitation of use endorsement or have a distance surcharge added without a limitation of use endorsement, it is usually better to pay the surcharge rather than limit the coverage. Again, most companies negotiate coverage and cost based on operations and will not attach limitation endorsements.

4. Watch Weight Classifications

The fourth variable in rating commercial automobiles is the *gross weight* of the vehicle, usually based on the manufacturer's capacity rating.

The logic behind this approach is that the heavier the vehicle, the more damage it can cause. Heavy vehicles also cost more to repair. Therefore, owners of heavier vehicles pay more in premiums.

This sounds very simple, but quite a few errors can be made. The business manager must be certain that the underwriter gets proper weight information. A common error occurs when a large truck becomes unreliable and is removed from its primary service. The configuration of the truck might be changed so that it can be used as an on-premises vehicle or in some similar operation. This is especially true of remanufactured vehicles whose weight capacity is changed because the cargo-carrying capability has been reconfigured. Again, in this area, if underwriters are not sure of the vehicle's actual weight, they assume higher weight levels and charge higher premiums.

Importance of Classifications. Figure 2.1 is taken from a typical insurance rating manual that contains scheduled factors for classification rating. Examining the table gives an idea of the cost variations that might occur due to misclassifications. If we assume that a base liability coverage rate for a heavy truck is $300, the rate gets modified by a factor from the schedule, depending on use and distance. For example, if it qualifies as a service vehicle which is used locally (under 50 miles), a 1.10 factor is applied to develop a premium of $330.

However, an underwriter might find this vehicle subject to the intermediate mileage charge (51 to 200 miles) and consider it a commercial vehicle. This intermediate distance surcharge, combined with a change in the vehicle's "use" category, demands a 2.25 factor that makes the premium $675. This example graphically illustrates the magnitude of savings to be realized by paying attention to these classifications. Remember, the territory classification variable might create a greater saving.

Most commercial insurance buyers do not understand or remember all these rating techniques. However, understanding the fundamentals allows the buyer to ask important questions of the insurance producer or company. There is really nothing magical about this approach, but buyers must pay particular attention to all details to get optimum cost and coverage.

The primary point to remember is that cost is *negotiable*. The more the underwriters know about your particular business, the more secure they will feel about taking risks and charging reasonable premiums.

5. Avoid Premiums on Mobile Equipment

The commercial general liability (CGL) policy insures against property damage and bodily injury liability arising out of the operation, owner-

NEW YORK (31)

COMMERCIAL LINES MANUAL
DIVISION ONE—AUTOMOBILE
EXCEPTION PAGE

| 37. TRUCKS, TRACTORS AND TRAILERS CLASSIFICATIONS | (Continued)

5. NON-FLEET PRIMARY CLASSIFICATIONS—RATING FACTORS AND STATISTICAL CODES

Size Class	Business Use Class		Radius Class					
			Local Up to 50 Miles		Intermediate 51 to 200 Miles		Long Distance Over 200 Miles	
			Liability	Phys. Dam.	Liability	Phys. Dam.	Liability	Phys. Dam.
Light Trucks (0-10,000 lbs G.V.W.)	Service	Factor	1.00	1.00	1.10	1.05	1.15	1.10
		Code	011——	011——	012——	012——	013——	013——
	Retail	Factor	1.60	1.20	1.65	1.50	1.70	1.65
		Code	021——	021——	022——	022——	023——	023——
	Commercial	Factor	1.30	1.15	1.55	1.40	1.60	1.70
		Code	031——	031——	032——	032——	033——	033——
							ZONE RATED	
Medium Trucks (10,001-20,000 lbs. G.V.W.)	Service	Factor	1.05	.85	1.20	1.00	.95	.95
		Code	211——	211——	212——	212——	213——	213——
	Retail	Factor	1.65	1.00	1.70	1.25	.95	.95
		Code	221——	221——	222——	222——	223——	223——
	Commercial	Factor	1.35	.95	1.60	1.20	.95	.95
		Code	231——	231——	232——	232——	233——	233——
Heavy Trucks (20,001-45,000 lbs. G.V.W.)	Service	Factor	1.10	.75	1.35	.85	1.00	1.00
		Code	311——	311——	312——	312——	313——	313——
	Retail	Factor	1.70	1.15	1.75	1.35	1.00	1.00
		Code	321——	321——	322——	322——	323——	323——
	Commercial	Factor	1.80	1.00	2.25	1.20	1.00	1.00
		Code	331——	331——	332——	332——	333——	333——
Extra-Heavy Trucks (Over 45,000 lbs. G.V.W.)		Factor	2.50	1.15	3.00	1.35	1.10	1.10
		Code	401——	401——	402——	402——	403——	403——
Heavy Trucks-Tractors (0-45,000 lbs. G.C.W.)	Service	Factor	1.50	1.05	1.55	1.15	1.00	1.00
		Code	341——	341——	342——	342——	343——	343——
	Retail	Factor	2.40	1.45	2.45	1.65	1.00	1.00
		Code	351——	351——	352——	352——	353——	353——
	Commercial	Factor	2.10	1.25	2.60	1.45	1.00	1.00
		Code	361——	361——	362——	362——	363——	363——
Extra-Heavy Truck-Tractors (Over 45,000 lbs. G.C.W.)		Factor	2.60	1.25	3.75	1.45	1.10	1.10
		Code	501——	501——	502——	502——	503——	503——
Trailer Types								
	Semitrailers	Factor	.25	.85	.30	1.05	.15	1.00
		Code	671——	671——	672——	672——	673——	673——
	Trailers	Factor	.15	.65	.30	.85	.15	1.00
		Code	681——	681——	682——	682——	683——	683——
Service or Utility Trailer (0-2,000 lbs. Load Capacity)		Factor	0	.40	0	.60	0	1.00
		Code	691——	691——	692——	692——	693——	693——

Figure 2.1 . Example of automobile distance use factors. (*Source: Insurance Services Office, Inc. Used with permission.*)

ship, and use of *mobile equipment,* just as the auto policy insures against liability from autos. However, no additional premium is charged in the CGL to cover individual units. As will be seen in Chapter 3, other types of exposure indicators are used in the CGL rating process. Since the auto policy makes a specific liability insurance charge for each vehicle and the CGL policy does not include a unit charge for mobile equipment, the distinction between "autos" and "mobile equipment" is important.

Mobile equipment is specifically and precisely defined in both the CGL and the auto policy. The definition is shown in Figure 2.2. Mistakes are often made in determining what vehicles are mobile equipment and what vehicles are autos. Unnecessary auto liability premiums are often paid as a result of these mistakes.

As Figure 2.2 shows, most construction and farm equipment gets classified as mobile equipment, as does a truck or automobile maintained and used solely on or next to owned premises. Trucks and

---

"Mobile equipment" means any of the following types of land vehicles, including any attached machinery or equipment:

a. Bulldozers, farm machinery, forklifts and other vehicles designed for use principally off public roads;

b. Vehicles maintained for use solely on or next to premises you own or rent;

c. Vehicles that travel on crawler treads;

d. Vehicles, whether self-propelled or not, maintained primarily to provide mobility to permanently mounted:
   (1) Power cranes, shovels, loaders, diggers or drills; or
   (2) Road construction or resurfacing equipment such as graders, scrapers or rollers;

e. Vehicles not described in a., b., c. or d. above that are not self-propelled and are maintained primarily to provide mobility to permanently attached equipment of the following types:
   (1) Air compressors, pumps and generators, including spraying, welding, building cleaning, geophysical exploration, lighting and well servicing equipment; or
   (2) Cherry pickers and similar devices used to raise or lower workers;

f. Vehicles not described in a., b., c. or d. above maintained primarily for purposes other than the transportation of persons or cargo.

However, self-propelled vehicles with the following types of permanently attached equipment are not "mobile equipment" but will be considered "autos":

(1) Equipment designed primarily for:
   (*a*) Snow removal;
   (*b*) Road maintenance, but not construction or resurfacing;
   (*c*) Street cleaning;

(2) Cherry pickers and similar devices mounted on automobile or truck chassis and used to raise or lower workers; and

(3) Air compressors, pumps and generators, including spraying, welding, building cleaning, geophysical exploration, lighting and well servicing equipment.

Figure 2.2. Mobile equipment definition. (*Source: Insurance Services Office, Inc., copyright ©1982, 1984, 1985. Used with permission.*)

similar vehicles that are maintained primarily to move power cranes and other specified equipment—as well as street and road construction or resurfacing equipment—get classified as mobile equipment. Likewise, air compressors, pumps, and the other items mentioned in Figure 2.2, paragraph $e(1)$ are considered mobile equipment even when mounted on trailers.

The insured should carefully review the automobile schedule to determine whether auto liability premiums are being paid on mobile equipment. Correction of such errors may eliminate a considerable amount of liability premiums. A word of caution: the commercial general liability policy does not insure against physical damage to the mobile equipment. (See cost recommendation 6 for a review of that area.)

6. Use Contractors Equipment Floater Policies

Mobile equipment such as that in cost recommendation 5 may be insured against physical damage in a contractors equipment policy. This policy can cover both the vehicle and the specialized equipment mounted upon it.

Oftentimes, automobile physical damage rates will run between 2 to 3 percent of the market value of the unit in question. If it qualifies, however, this equipment may be covered under a contractors equipment policy for a rate ranging between $.60 to $1.25 per $100 of value. This is a substantial savings over using the automobile policy for such coverage. Generally, the more equipment that can be moved from the auto policy and insured under a contractors equipment policy, the lower the premium cost will be.

7. Recognize "On-Premises" and Industrial Vehicles

Many businesses have vehicles that are used primarily on premises. For example, a contractor or manufacturer might keep a flatbed truck primarily to transport materials or equipment on premises, but occasional use over the road could prevent its being classified as mobile equipment.

Many state laws require that these vehicles be licensed. Just because a given piece of equipment may be operated off premises occasionally does not necessarily mean that premiums should be the same as those paid on a vehicle used regularly on the roads. As a result, a provision in the insurance rating manuals stipulates that a nominal premium charge can be made for such "industrial" vehicles. For example, an old truck, equipped with gin poles and a winder, is normally used on premises; however, it may leave the insured's premises and go down the street to a storage location. For this incidental "over-the-road" exposure, the industrial rate should apply.

8. Get Personal Vehicle Rating Credits

Privately owned companies often furnish vehicles to spouses or others and insure them under the business auto policy. If the major use of these vehicles is for nonbusiness purposes, the insurance company will sometimes agree to classify them as being for personal use and charge rates much lower than those applied to commercial vehicles.

9. Reduce Recreational Vehicle Premiums

Many corporations own recreational vehicles such as campers, hunting vehicles, and the like. Obviously, if the vehicles are garaged in an urban area and designated in a high-use category, the premium can be quite high. It is often possible to garage them in the rural areas where they are used and have them classified as farm vehicles to establish a lower premium.

10. Consider Fire, Theft, and Specified Causes-of-Loss Coverage

As mentioned at the beginning of this chapter, *comprehensive coverage* is one of two types of physical damage insurance usually provided by the policy for owned autos. Comprehensive covers any and all perils that might damage the automobile except collision, overturn, and certain excluded perils. The coverage is *all risk* and will even cover damage caused in very unusual situations such as an oil well's spewing acid that eats away the paint, the dog's getting upset and ripping the upholstery, or a sandstorm's sandblasting the windows. As one might expect, this coverage is fairly expensive.

Fire, theft, and specified causes of loss (formerly called *specified perils*) coverage, are an alternative approach to insuring comprehensive. This is *named perils coverage*, which provides protection against specified perils such as:

- Fire
- Theft

- Windstorm

- Hail

- Smoke

- Explosion

- Flood

- Vandalism

- Damage by airplane or falling objects

It is substantially less expensive than comprehensive coverage.

Exposures not covered will be very unusual, seldom occurring events such as those mentioned earlier. In addition, damage to windshields from flying rocks, often encountered on roadways, would be excluded. If there is low exposure to these perils or if the insured can afford to retain some of the exposure, such as windshield damage, this approach should be used. In most cases, the alternative named perils coverage will save substantial dollars in insurance premiums.

To analyze the potential savings, obtain alternative quotes for comprehensive and for fire, theft, and specified perils. If the premium difference is large enough, you can assume some reasonable risk which will not be large enough to cause financial hardship.

11. Use Deductibles

Deductibles may be assumed for collision, comprehensive, and even the bodily injury and property damage liability coverage. With respect to collision and comprehensive, some minimum deductibles are normally required. Therefore, under these coverages, the question is not really whether to take the deductible but how much of a deductible to assume. It is usually beneficial to assume a $500 collision deductible on private passenger automobiles and pickups and up to a $1,000 deductible on larger vehicles. On larger fleets, even higher collision deductibles may be desirable.

Determining Deductible Levels. The best approach for determining the optimum amount of deductible to assume is simply to analyze the premium savings. Compare premium credits for assuming a larger deductible with the dollar value of the expected additional loss assumption based on past losses. Obviously, any change in the size of the fleet affects this analysis.

The basic loss analysis should be similar to the following example. Let's assume that your firm wants to determine whether to go from a

$250 collision deductible to a $500 on private passenger vehicles. Let's also suppose that this will save $1,000 in premium for these particular vehicles.

Past experience shows that at least two accidents over $500 should occur during the year. This means an additional $500 (2 × $250) in deductible expense is expected to be sustained. Therefore, if $1,000 in premium is saved and an additional $500 is assumed in higher deductibles, a net $500 of savings will be realized in addition to the investment income on the $1,000 of premiums not paid to the insurance company. This savings merits shifting to a higher deductible.

The same analysis can be applied to comprehensive coverage. The shift from a $100 comprehensive deductible to a $250 comprehensive deductible will probably be well worth the increase in loss assumption. Similar benefits may be available for assuming higher deductibles for fire, theft, and specified causes-of-loss coverage.

On larger fleets, you should consider moving to an annual aggregate deductible program. This provides that the insured will pay deductibles up to an annual aggregate level, say $50,000, and after that, the insurance company will reimburse all losses. Often, this annual aggregate deductible program can be expanded to cover nonautomotive equipment (e.g., contractor's equipment) as well.

Liability Deductibles. Deductibles may also be used with liability coverages. With respect to bodily injury, however, the deductible credit is often not large enough to warrant the risk. Also, underwriters worry that the insured may fail to promptly report a potentially severe claim, initially believing that no injury occurred; therefore, many insurers will not allow a bodily injury liability deductible. However, property damage liability deductibles can save a considerable amount of money, especially deductibles in the range of $250 to $2,500. Every insured who owns more than five vehicles should seriously consider assuming at least a $250 property damage liability deductible.

An interesting twist to liability deductibles is that the insured does not have to adjust its own claims below the deductible level. Claims can be handled on a "contributory basis." The insurance company will settle the claim and then bill the insured for the deductible. This approach avoids the problem of adjusting and researching the claim. However, insurance companies may resist this approach because they are highly computerized and may want to avoid the additional accounting caused by "backcharging" the insured for the deductible portion.

One word of caution about liability insurance deductibles—there are two types:

1. "Per occurrence" basis deductibles

2. "Per claim" basis deductibles

A *per occurrence* basis deductible applies only one time for all claims arising from a particular accident. For example, consider a highway accident involving 12 automobiles, caused by a company employee. The per occurrence property damage liability deductible of, for instance, $500 would apply only once to the accident.

On the other hand, a *per claim* basis deductible would apply to each of the 12 claims. In other words, the insured would have to pay $6,000 in deductibles instead of $500. Of course, per claim deductibles provide greater reductions of premiums than per occurrence deductibles. However, the potentially higher retained deductibles must be considered. Small businesses should probably stick to the per occurrence basis deductibles.

In summary, deductibles should be strongly considered in the areas of physical damage and property damage liability. A loss analysis combined with alternative premium quotes can usually determine whether the use of higher deductibles can be cost-effective in the long run.

12. Self-Insure Collision

As the number of owned vehicles increases, self-insurance of collision becomes more desirable, especially for vehicles more than 3 years old. Many managers will seriously consider self-insurance when premiums equal the average value of owned vehicles. It is quite improbable that more than one owned vehicle will be involved in a single collision. Therefore, collision is a good area to self-insure. An analysis identical to that used in selecting a collision deductible can be used to determine the feasibility of insuring collision.

Some firms will continue to purchase collision coverage on new vehicles but will drop this coverage after 2 or 3 years. This approach assumes that the vehicle's value will approach the sum of the premium and the deductible after 2 or 3 years.

Another approach is to determine the amount of loss a particular firm can assume and then only insure those vehicles for collision over and beyond the determined self-insurance limit. However, it should be recognized that more than one collision can occur in a particular year, and past experience must be considered.

Self-insurance with respect to fire, theft, specified causes of loss, and/or comprehensive coverage should normally be avoided by all but the largest organizations. Vehicles are often garaged together during off-hours or on weekends; as a result, many owned vehicles can be damaged by a single event such as a fire, an explosion, or a hailstorm.

The aggregate losses in such an event could far exceed the premium savings. However, organizations that have large fleets spread over many states may want to look at self-insurance of this exposure as well as collision.

13. Obtain Schedule Credits/Debits and Dividends

Thus far, this chapter has discussed the development of *manual premium,* the premium determined solely by applying the rules and factors specified in the industry's rating manuals.

Once an insurance underwriter has determined the manual premiums for automobile liability and physical damage, the premiums can be further adjusted by applying schedule credits or debits. Usually, these range from a 25 percent discount up to a 25 percent debit (surcharge). In some states, particularly Texas, such flexibility is not allowed. However, insurance companies have the option of paying dividends on premiums in the range of 10 to 15 percent. Subjective factors often used in developing a credit or debit (surcharge) include:

- Motor vehicle records (MVRs)
- Prior loss experience
- Age of vehicles
- Driver selection and training program
- Vehicle maintenance program
- Percent of young and old drivers to total number of drivers
- Weather conditions common to area
- Vehicles driven in urban versus rural areas
- Types of terrain traveled

The insurance buyer should review these factors, determine whether cost-effective improvements can be made, and make sure that all positive factors are communicated to the underwriter. During a "buyer's market," insurance is readily available and insurance companies are competing for the consumer's premium dollar. In such times, schedule credits are fairly easy to obtain. When the market begins to tighten, a "seller's market" develops and buyers will see their schedule credits disappear; they may be subject to debits instead. While the application of schedule rating may fluctuate based upon the existing market, many underwriters continue to use this rating approach in a logical fashion. Therefore, the buyer should ascertain the credits or surcharges being currently applied and the basis for them. If the maximum 25 percent credit is not being applied, then underwriters should be asked what the buyer must do to obtain the maximum credit. Understanding this important rating factor can substantially reduce net costs over the long term.

14. Use Experience Rating

Most business managers are familiar with the application of experience rating with respect to unemployment insurance administered by the government and most states. In two jurisdictions, Texas and Louisiana, experience rating of automobile liability is mandatory after a business has been in existence for 2 years if the premium is more than $7,000. Even though these state plans are conservative, the insurance buyer can develop reasonable credits if lower than average losses have been incurred.

Outside Texas and Louisiana, such plans are not mandatory. Although the Insurance Services Office publishes a guideline plan, each insurance company adopts its own modified program. The modified factors used by the insurance companies will become more or less competitive as the status of the insurance market changes. If an organization has few losses, additional discounts may be added to the scheduled credit approach. In a soft market, credits of 35 to 50 percent (schedule and experience rating combined) off the manual rate are not uncommon. For extremely large risks, credits will even be larger. If the underwriter views past loss experience as unsatisfactory, experience rating will develop substantial surcharges. Often, this past bad experience can be mitigated by assuming deductibles. Although the experience rating is calculated using reduced premiums (i.e., premiums after deductible credits), the deductible is subtracted from losses. If the deductible eliminates a larger dollar amount of losses than the deductible credit reduces the premium used in the calculation, the net effect will be an even greater savings than just the deductible credit.

15. Use the Suspension of Insurance Endorsement

Liability and physical damage rates generally contemplate year-round use of a vehicle, but some vehicles may not be used year-round due to the seasonal nature of operations. For instance, an ice plant may store some vehicles during the winter. Another example might be a street contractor who uses his vehicles only during the warmer months. Other situations may involve slowdowns of a particular business or labor strikes that force equipment to be taken out of service.

In any event, if the automobiles are not being used, the insured can save money by suspending the insurance coverage on these vehicles while they are out of service if such period exceeds 30 days.

Once a piece of equipment has been out of service for more than 30 days, the insurance buyer can negotiate credits on the premium rates for that particular automobile for the period of time during which the automobile has been out of service. The buyer may negotiate a direct return or can be reimbursed through schedule credits.

The policy is usually endorsed for this inactivity in some way, to indicate that coverage has been suspended. Of course, if an accident does occur, no coverage is provided. As a result, great care must be taken to prevent a loss by making sure the equipment is not used.

Automobiles on which coverage is suspended should be scheduled under the general liability policy as "mobile equipment." This will provide liability (not physical damage) coverage should someone somehow be injured by the vehicle or should an employee inadvertently drive the vehicle and have an accident.

In summary, if full rates are presently being paid for automobiles that are not used the entire year, credits may be negotiated to reflect the suspension of insurance. One caveat: while liability and collision coverage may be suspended, be sure to continue the comprehensive or fire, theft, and specified causes of loss coverage to avoid uninsured physical damage that may occur while the automobiles are in storage.

16. Understand the "Stated Amount" Approach

The normal procedure for rating an automobile is to apply depreciation factors to the original, new cost of the vehicle. This is called the *actual cash value*. The depreciation factor is determined by the age group classification for a given vehicle. Basically, as a vehicle gets older, the rates get lower. However, with respect to fire, theft, and specified causes of loss coverage or comprehensive coverage, there is an alternative approach. The insured can request coverage on a *stated amount* basis. For vehicles with a long life, this approach might be desirable so as to avoid the minimal depreciation amounts used under the actual cash value approach. For instance, if a truck's new cost is $75,000 and the actual cash value is based on a lower amount of depreciation than the insured thinks is appropriate, the insured might elect to use the stated amount basis. Under this arrangement, a higher depreciation factor can be used to reduce the insured value. The insurance rates will then be applied to a lower stated value, resulting in a net lower premium.

A word of caution: the insured can collect no more than the *lesser* of the stated amount or the actual cash value in the event of a loss. This can cause a problem in times of severe inflation, when the replacement cost of the vehicle may be much higher. However, unless the entire vehicle is subject to a *total* loss, such as by theft, this should be of no great concern. Therefore, the maximum probable loss is related more to the cost of a partial loss than the cost of a total loss.

Usually, the savings produced by this approach are not enough to justify the effort to employ it if only three or four vehicles are involved. For large fleets of vehicles, however, this type of coverage may be appropriate. In summary, if vehicles are over 5 years old and have a substantially high new cost, the stated amount approach may save a great deal of money.

17. Discontinue Medical Payments and Personal Injury Protection

Because of concern over injury to customers and employees, many businesses choose to buy medical payments coverage as well as personal injury protection for their commercial vehicles (nonprivate passenger vehicles). This coverage pays the cost of medical care after an accident incurred by nonemployees who are passengers in the automobile and is in addition to any claims paid to these persons under the bodily injury liability coverage.

In general, medical payments coverage is advisable for a family automobile. For commercial risks, though, the story is different. Losses which generally range from $2,500 to $5,000 in this category will be considered in arriving at rates and premiums in future policy periods. For that reason, a $2,000 loss paid under this coverage would generate a premium in later years which could approach $4,000 to $5,000. Since the limits are very low on this coverage and the exposures are not that great, it may be better to pay the losses if and when they occur rather than have the insurance company pay them and then increase the premiums in later periods. In many cases, the payments will be made on behalf of nonemployees or customers. Depending on the circumstances, the insured may feel no responsibility for the injuries and elect not to pay the medical expenses. Self-insurance preserves the option with the insured. Employees will be covered under workers compensation or group medical insurance.

Therefore, it may be best not to insure this exposure. If someoneriding in the owned vehicle has no workers compensation or hospitalization coverage, a situation which will be very rare, then it is best for the business to pay the loss out of its own pocket. The payment by the company would be well received and would definitely save premiums down the road.

18. Drop Uninsured Motorists Coverage Where Possible

Many states will allow the business to reject uninsured motorists coverage. This coverage applies when the insured vehicle is involved with an uninsured or hit-and-run motorist. The insured can then sue its own insurance company as if its insurance company were the insurance carrier for the other motorist.

First of all, it's not much fun to sue your own insurance company. Moreover, in most cases, this coverage does not provide very high limits. Also, uninsured motorists coverage does not apply if workers compensation insurance covers the injury. Again, this coverage is good for family autos but should usually not be purchased for commercial vehicles. If desirable, savings in this area can be used to improve health and accident coverages to remove any negative ramifications for dropping this coverage. An exception to this point might be in those states which allow high limits of uninsured motorists coverage.

19. Think Twice about Rental Car Collision Waivers

When renting a vehicle, you are given an option to accept or decline the collision waiver. Acceptance of this coverage means the collision deductible of $250 to $1,500 will be waived. People often assume that this option is to purchase collision coverage subject to some deductible rather than simply to waive the deductible.

The rental payments usually include standard collision coverage and simply require an additional amount of money to waive the deductible. If the premium charge is multiplied by 365 days, the annual premium may equal as much as 5 times the coverage limit being purchased. If a company is willing to assume the deductible in its own fleet policy, it would do well to take the same approach for rental cars. Exceptions might be where the cost of the collision waiver could be passed back to a customer, as in a law firm or an accounting firm that is reimbursed for expenses, or where the collision deductible would exceed some predetermined amount, such as $1,000.

At the same time, accident and health insurance coverage should be rejected. Coverage for this area is provided by the organization's workers compensation and/or employee benefits program. In summary, all the additional rental coverages should usually be rejected by medium-sized and large businesses unless there is a specific reason to do otherwise. Small businesses that do not frequently rent vehicles should review the rental agreement and purchase the collision waiver if the deductible is greater than some prespecified amount (e.g., $500).

20. Self-Insure Auto Liability

Self-insurance of bodily injury and property damage liability is an alternative for large organizations and may lead to substantial savings. It should be noted, however, that many states have financial responsibility laws requiring the organization to buy insurance. In those states, the organization can file with regulatory authorities, usually the state board of insurance or insurance commissioner, to become a qualified self-insurer. To become a qualified self-insurer, the prospective self-insured must meet certain minimum qualifications. If self-insurance of this exposure is under consideration, allow adequate time for regulatory approval.

Because of the catastrophic loss potential of auto liability, only the low levels of loss (e.g., the first $100,000 to $1 million) should be assumed. Excess insurance should be purchased above this level. Obviously, this alternative is only for large organizations, and statistical analysis of past loss experience can be helpful in determining the optimum retention level.

3
Commercial General Liability Insurance

The commercial general liability (CGL) policy (1986 edition) protects the organization against lawsuits alleging bodily injury or property damage legal liability. In other words, the policy insures against defense costs, awards, or settlements associated with lawsuits brought by third parties who are injured by the insured's premises operations, products-completed operations, or independent contractors. The policy also automatically includes contractual liability insurance which causes it to provide protection to other parties whom the insured agrees in a business contract to "hold harmless and indemnify."

Coverage Triggers

This coverage for bodily injury and property damage liability may be on an *occurrence* or *claims-made* basis. These two terms relate to the triggering event that must happen for the policy to apply. Traditionally, CGL policies have been on an occurrence basis. With this type of insurance, the organization has coverage for any liability arising from injuries or damages that occur while the policy is in force. On the other hand, with claims-made insurance, a policy must be in force when the claim is made. While there are some protective safeguards included in claims-made forms, this approach can result in significant coverage gaps if a policy is not in force when a claim is made. Business managers should make certain they understand all the implications of claims-made insurance and negotiate into the policy the broadest possible protective safeguards before buying CGL coverage on this basis. For more information on claims-made insurance, see Appendix A.

Personal and Advertising Injury Coverage

In addition to coverage for bodily injury and property damage liability, the policy extends to provide "personal injury and advertising injury" liability coverage. The personal injury portion of this insurance protects against suits brought by others alleging libel, slander, defamation of character, false arrest, disparagement of goods, and similar allegations. The advertising injury coverage insures against disparagement of goods, slander, copyright infringement, and similar allegations which may arise in connection with the advertising activities of the organization. As a word of caution, however, this advertising liability coverage applies only to organizations advertising their own products; it does not provide errors and omissions coverage for advertising agencies, publishers, or broadcasters.

Medical Payments Coverage

The policy also provides a type of "no fault" medical payments coverage. This coverage will reimburse the insured for medical bills paid on behalf of others who are injured on the insured's premises or by the insured's operations subject to a $5,000 per person limit. Taking this approach to medical expenses is thought to reduce the likelihood that injured parties will bring a lawsuit.

Classifications and Rating

As in other lines of insurance, the *manual premium* for the CGL policy is determined by multiplying an appropriate manual rate by the number of exposure units. Therefore, the first step in determining the manual premium is to calculate the appropriate rate. This involves properly classifying the insured's operations, finding the corresponding rate, and adjusting this rate with regard to the desired limits of liability.

Once a classification has been selected, the next step is to find the rate associated with that classification. An individual insurer may develop its own rates or join with others by subscribing to rates developed by

Insurance Services Office (ISO). Such insurers may modify these "bureau" rates but will often use them as a starting point.

Finally, since the bureau rates are based on limits of liability of only $25,000 each "occurrence" for bodily injury and property damage, $25,000 per person or organization for personal injury and advertising injury, and $50,000 general aggregate and products/completed operations aggregate limits, they must be adjusted for the higher limits of liability usually purchased. This is accomplished by multiplying the "basic limits rate" by an appropriate "increase limits factor" which is found in a table in the rating manual. Mistakes that may lead to premium overcharges can be made in choosing classification codes and/or the amount of the exposure base to use in rating the policy; they can also be made in applying certain other rating rules, discussed in the following "Ways to Control Costs."

Ways to Control Costs

This chapter gives you 17 ways to control general liability insurance costs.

21. Use Proper Classifications

The first step in rating a commercial general liability (CGL) policy is to determine the classification which *best* describes the insured's business operations. The purpose of the classification system is to group insureds with similar operations together in order to facilitate a statistical analysis of losses so that rates can be determined for all insureds in that business class. As can be seen in Table 3.1, there are four general categories of classification codes: mercantile, manufacturing, buildings, and contracting. In addition, there is a "miscellaneous" category which includes various types of codes that do not fit into the four primary classification groupings. Each individual classification is assigned a unique classification code number within the rating manuals published by ISO. Figure

Table 3.1 CGL Classifications Summary

Industry group	Numerical sequence	Exposure base
Mercantile	10000–19999	Gross sales*
Manufacturing/processing	50000–59999	Gross sales*
Buildings/premises	60000–69999	Area, units, or gross sales*
Contracting/servicing	90000–99999	Payroll*
Miscellaneous	40,000–49,999	Various

*These exposure bases usually apply on a per 1,000 basis.

3.1 gives some examples of these classification codes. The rate for a particular classification code within a particular state can be determined by simply looking up the classification code in the "state rate pages." Rates are then adjusted to reflect increases in policy limits and multiplied by the exposure base. Note that the exposure base is usually on a per 1,000 basis, meaning that the actual amount of sales, area, or payroll is divided by 1,000 before being multiplied by the rate.

An insurance buyer should spend time with the agent or broker studying the classification code(s) used to rate the organization's CGL. Carefully consider the business operations and the extent to which they fit within the scope of the classification code. In particular, look for classification codes that carry lower rates which might be more appropriate for the organization's operations. In addition, more than one classification code may be applicable if the organization has multiple business operations. For example, a manufacturer that makes both powered and unpowered hand tools would rate its business with two classification codes: 59782, "tool manufacturing—hand type—not powered"; and 59783, "tool manufacturing—hand type—powered." The

DESCRIPTION	Fire and allied lines	Multiple line			Conts. BP Fire or CPP Rate Group	General liability		Crime			For company use
	Class code	CPP PMA	BP Class code	BP Rate no.		Class code	Premium base	Class code	Rate group	Class limit	
Building material dealers	(1)	M	52114	2	4	10255 (2)	s	5210	1 (3)	2,000	
Building material dealers — second-hand material	(1)	M	52114	2	4	10256 (4)	s	5210	1 (3)	2,000	
Building material distributors	(1)	M		NA	4	10257 (5)	s	5210	1 (3)	2,000	
Building structure — raising or moving	(6)	(6)		NA	4	91280 (7)	P	1700	2	7,500	
Buildings or premises — bank or office	0702	0	(8)	(8)	(9)	61215 NOC (10)(11) (17)	a+	6500	2 (12)	3,000	
Buildings or premises — bank or office — mercantile or manufacturing (lessor's risk only)	(13)	(13)	(14)		(9)	61211 (10)(15)	a+	NA			
Buildings or premises — bank or office — mercantile or manufacturing — maintained by the insured (lessor's) risk only	(13)	(13)	(14)		(9)	61213 (10)	a+	NA			
Buildings or premises — bank or office — premises occupied by employees of	(13)	(13)		NA	(9)	61214 (10)(11) (16)(17)	a+	6500	2 (12)	2,000	

Figure 3.1. Illustrative commercial lines classification codes. (*Source: Insurance Services Office, Inc. Used with permission.*)

difference in the products and completed-operations rate for these two classification codes can be substantial, and it may be to the insured's benefit to separate the two types of products for rating purposes.

22. Use Lessor's Risk Only Classification

When an organization owns a building and leases a substantial amount of that building to other businesses, the organization's liability exposures arising from that premises are reduced because the tenants will carry liability insurance for their portions of the building. The owner should also insert a *hold harmless* clause into the lease agreement whereby the tenants hold the owner of the building harmless for liability arising from their parts of the premises as well as their operations. In conjunction with the hold harmless clause, the lease should require the tenants to purchase general liability insurance, including contractual liability coverage.

In recognition of the reduced exposures associated with these actions, a substantial rate credit is available to insureds who occupy less than 90 percent of an owned building. The portion of the premises occupied by the insured is classified and rated according to the insured's business operations. The remainder of the premises falls under one of two classification codes: "buildings or premises—bank or office—mercantile or manufacturing (lessor's risk only)," code number 61211; or "buildings or premises—bank or office—mercantile or manufacturing—maintained by the insured (lessor's risk only)," code number 61213.

These two classifications carry a much lower rate than the regular "buildings or premises" codes. For example, the basic limits rate (occurrence coverage) for code 61211 in North Carolina at the time of this writing is $6.27 versus a rate of $35.40 per 1,000 square feet for code 61215, "buildings or premises—bank or office." As can be seen, substantial premium savings can be obtained through the use of this rating rule.

23. Delete Truck Drivers' and Pilots' Payrolls

Contractors and service companies whose exposure base is *payroll* should not include the payroll of drivers and their helpers whose primary duties are to work in or on automobiles or trucks. The liability exposure is connected with the activities of these individuals, i.e., driving is insured by the automobile policy rather than the general liability policy (which excludes liability arising from owned autos), and these payrolls are therefore not included in the exposure base for general liability insurance. For the same reason, wages paid to aircraft pilots and copilots whose principal duties involve work on or in connection with aircraft are not included in the payroll used as an exposure base for general liability insurance.

24. Delete Clerical Office Employees' Payrolls

Contractors and other service providers for which *payroll* is used as the exposure base should not include the payroll of clerical office employees. This rule applies only if these employees are physically separated from other work areas of the insured and if their duties are strictly clerical in nature.

25. Delete Overtime Surcharges

Extra pay for overtime is also not included in the payroll of contractors and other service providers for which *payroll* is used as an exposure base. In other words, the extra 50 percent of the hourly wage paid to an employee who works overtime is not included in the payroll exposure base. This rule does not apply to stevedores, and to use it for other classifications, the insured must maintain records to indicate overtime pay separately by employee and in summary by classification code. For many insureds, this additional record-keeping requirement will be more than justified by the dollar premium savings.

26. Use Executive Officer Payroll Limitation

For contractors and other servicing organizations whose exposure base is *payroll*, the payroll of executive officers, individual owners, and partners is included in the exposure base. However, most states limit the amount of payroll for each of these individuals who is included. For example, at the time of this writing, North Dakota includes only the first $24,200 of annual individual payroll for each executive officer. In New Mexico, only the first $27,900 is included at this time. Make certain that limited payroll amounts for executive officers are included rather than the entire amount of the annual salary for each officer. Your insurance agent or broker should be able to specify the payroll limitation in the state(s) where operations are conducted.

27. Look Twice at Intercompany Sales

The CGL policy will cover a suit against one insured brought by another insured. For this reason, the money paid to one company by a sister company for goods or products is included in the *gross sales* exposure base of insureds in the manufacturing/processing or mercantile businesses. This coverage for intercompany suits can, however, be excluded by endorsement. When this is done, intercompany sales will be deleted from the applicable exposure base.

It is suggested that the business manager determine what dollar volume of intercompany sales is being included in the general liability exposure base. The ultimate effect on premium can be determined by multiplying the applicable rate times the intercompany sales amount divided by 1,000. The exposure to intercompany suits and the need for general liability insurance coverage by one organization being sued by another should then be analyzed. Many organizations with subsidiaries will not feel the need to cover the liability suits brought by one subsidiary against the other subsidiary and will be willing to exclude coverage in return for a lower premium expenditure.

28. Delete Sales Taxes and Excise Taxes

For those organizations rated using a gross sales exposure base, sales and excise taxes paid to governmental entities should not be included in the exposure base. In a similar vein, finance charges for items sold on an installment basis are also not included in the exposure base.

29. Take Advantage of the Transition Program

With the introduction of the 1986 CGL program, the premises and operations rating base for mercantile classifications was changed from an *area* to a *gross sales* basis. Similarly, the products and completed operations exposure base for contractors changed from *receipts* to *payroll*, and both the premises-operations and products-completed operations exposure bases for manufacturers changed from *payroll* and *receipts*, respectively, to *gross sales*. Without some type of limitation on the amount of premium change, a simple change in the rating base could result in a drastic increase or decrease in the applicable premium of a particular insured simply because of the change in rating base. For example, the general liability premium of a retail store with a high volume of sales and a relatively small amount of floor area could increase dramatically. A similar result would occur with a manufacturer that has a higher-than-average ratio of gross sales to payroll or receipts or with a contractor that has a higher-than-average ratio of payroll to receipts. To avoid dramatic increases or decreases in premiums as a result of only the change of exposure base, a "transition program" was devised.

The program applies only to classifications for which the exposure base was changed when the new CGL program was introduced. A transition program runs for 5 years following the changeover even if a change of insurance companies occurs during that 5-year period. If at any time during the 5-year transition program, the audit calculation, as specified in the ISO rating manual, shows that a classification or a location does not remain within the program, it is permanently removed from any further application of the transition program. Business managers with mercantile, construction, or manufacturing establishments should discuss this transition program with their agents and satisfy themselves that it has been properly applied.

30. Use Experience Rating

Experience rating of CGL insurance is optional in all states except Texas and Louisiana, where it's mandatory. It involves the use of a formula which compares the insured's past loss experience to that of other insureds with similar operations to calculate an experience modifier. The experience modifier is then applied to decrease or increase the manual premium. Typically, the insured must have an annual manual premium of $3,000 or more to be eligible for experience rating.

Experience rating tends to be more sensitive to loss frequency than to loss severity. In other words, for example, an insured with ten $5,000 losses would be penalized more than an insured with one $50,000 loss. Therefore, an insured that has experienced a low frequency of losses may be able to reduce general liability insurance costs by encouraging the underwriter to experience rate the premium.

31. Obtain Schedule Credit/Dividends

Schedule rating allows the underwriter to modify manual rates either upward (debits) or downward (credits) to reflect the individual risk characteristics of the insured. The characteristics generally given consideration for general liability insurance include:

- Care and condition of premises
- Geographic location

- Type of equipment used in operations, including maintenance
- Selection, training, supervision, and experience of employees
- Product quality control programs

In a few states, such as Texas, underwriters are not permitted to use schedule credits/debits. Underwriters in these states often have the option of paying dividends to general liability insurance policyholders. While it is to the insured's advantage to be eligible to receive dividends, it is important to remember that they cannot be guaranteed. Don't count on receiving a dividend until it has actually been paid.

32. Use Deductibles

As with other lines of insurance, the assumption of deductibles by the insured can significantly reduce the premium charged for coverage. Commercial general liability insurance can be written subject to a bodily injury liability deductible, a property damage liability deductible, or a combined bodily injury and property damage deductible. These deductibles can range in amount from $250 into the thousands of dollars. The deductibles may be written on either a *per claim* or *per occurrence* basis, with the per claim basis deductible providing the largest reduction of premium. However, keep in mind that a single accident can lead to the imposition of several per claim deductibles, whereas only one per occurrence deductible would apply. When looking at deductibles, always compare an estimate of the additional amount that will be paid in deductibles to the premium savings.

33. Negotiate Advisory (A) Rates

Even in states where rates are carefully regulated, some of the rates used for commercial general liability insurance are subject to the underwriter's discretion. These "advisory" (A) rates are filed with insurance regulators in many states, but underwriters are provided with the flexibility to vary from these filed rates. In states where rates are not heavily regulated, they are often not even filed with the state, and underwriters may use whatever rates they please. (A) rates are most prevalent in two areas: the rates used for products-completed operations liability coverage and the increased limits factors.

In a soft, buyer's marketplace, these rates can be negotiated downward to effect substantial cost savings. In a tight, seller's marketplace, however, underwriters will increase these (A) rates. The main point to keep in mind here is that general liability rates are negotiable, even in states with considerable rate regulation.

34. Negotiate Premium Credits for
Coverage Limitations

A number of insurance coverages currently included in the commercial general liability policy which, in previous years, had to be purchased for additional premiums can be deleted from the policy by exclusionary endorsements. The coverages that can be deleted from the policy by exclusionary endorsement include: blanket contractual liability, personal injury liability, advertising injury liability, medical payments coverage, fire legal liability, "explosion, collapse, and underground property damage," and employees as insureds. In a tight insurance marketplace, some underwriters may require the deletion of one or more of these coverages. While such coverage restrictions should be resisted, a fallback position might be to negotiate for reduced rates in recognition of the restricted coverage.

The insurance industry has not established any guideline rate credits to be applied when these coverage restrictions are imposed. Like advisory rates, these premium reductions are negotiable.

35. Drop Medical Payments
Coverage

One of the "fringe" coverages automatically provided by the commercial general liability policy that medium-sized and larger insureds should ask to have deleted from the policy is *medical payments coverage*. This coverage reimburses the insured for money expended in arranging for first aid or other medical treatment of third parties injured on an insured's premises. In effect, it is "goodwill" insurance. Any losses paid by the medical payments coverage will affect the insured's loss experience. In addition, of course, premiums are charged for this coverage. Deletion of the coverage from the policy should result in reduced premiums and will remove some claims from the loss experience.

While accidents would, of course, need to be reported to the insurer, the insured can decide whether or not to pay these medical expenses to injured individuals on a case-by-case basis when the coverage is not purchased. In many situations, they should be paid in order to preserve a customer relationship and/or reduce the customer's incentive to make a liability claim.

36. Think Twice about the
Claims-Made Option

There are two standard commercial general liability policies which are identical except for the "coverage trigger" mechanism. One of these policies is on the traditional *occurrence* basis, which means that the policy in effect at the time the covered bodily injury or property damage occurs will insure claims resulting from the injury or damage regardless of when the claims are made. The other policy is on a *claims-made* basis. This policy insures claims made during the policy period associated with injuries or damages which occurred on or after the specified "retroactive date" in the policy. To assure that there are no gaps in coverage, an insured can never stop purchasing claims-made insurance, and the retroactive date cannot be moved forward in time (or "tail coverage" must be purchased in either case). The occurrence and claims-made policies are explained in more detail in Appendix A, and this explanation should be carefully reviewed.

Since the imposition of a retroactive date places a time limitation on when injuries or damages must occur in order to be covered by the policy, a premium reduction is provided whenever the retroactive date is advanced (moved forward in time) to recognize the reduced amount of risk being insured. The amount of the premium reduction decreases each year for 5 years, after which it virtually disappears. In other words, the claims-made policy premium increases each year for 5 years. The rating manual calls for the application of a "claims-made multiplier" during the first 4 years to effect these discounts. A business manager should make certain that these discounts are provided whenever the retroactive date is advanced.

Because of the initial premium discounts provided in conjunction with a claims-made liability program, it would seem that switching from an occurrence to a claims-made program would be a good way to save money. However, these premium discounts should be considered not as permanent premium savings but rather as a deferral of premiums until a future date. If, in the future, the retroactive date is advanced, it will be necessary to pay additional premiums in order to procure extended reporting period ("tail") coverage. For example, the standard claims-made CGL policy drafted by ISO allows the insurer to charge up to 200 percent of the annual policy premium for its "supplemental extended reporting period" option. While the insurer cannot require the business manager to purchase this option, failure to do so may very well result in no coverage being applicable to some future liability claims.

Therefore, a move to claims-made insurance may result in a deferral of premiums until some future date. However, the time that those premiums will become payable, if ever, is substantially under the control of the underwriters. The "tail coverage" will be needed when the underwriter decides to cancel coverage, not to renew, or to advance the retroactive date. This is most likely to occur in tight insurance markets when the insurance buyer will have few, if any, other competitive alternatives than to buy the extended reporting period. In conclusion, the business manager should not switch to claims-made insurance for the sole reason of reducing premiums.

37. Obtain Certificates from Contractors

The CGL policy automatically covers suits brought against the insured because of the operations of its independent contractors. This is called *independent contractor's coverage.* A fairly low rate applies to this coverage, recognizing a reduced exposure because of the liability insurance carried by the contractors. However, the low rate applies only if the insured obtains proof that its contractors are carrying "adequate insurance." This is done by obtaining and keeping on file certificates of insurance showing that they have liability insurance. If certificates are not obtained, a much higher rate can be charged by the insurer when the annual audit is performed. To avoid this extra premium charge, all contractors and subcontractors should be required to purchase liability (and workers compensation) insurance and provide certificates of insurance showing such coverage is in place.

In addition to immediately avoiding the additional premium that can be charged by the insurer, requiring liability insurance from independent contractors, *and* including a hold harmless clause in the contract, will help insulate the organization's insurance from paying losses they cause. This preserves both the organization's liability limits, which can be very important when there is a major disaster and everyone involved has potential liabilities, and keeps claims that could cause future premium increases out of the organization's loss experience. At the minimum, require contractors to purchase "public liability insurance, including coverage for personal injury, bodily injury, property damage, completed operations, contractual liability. . ." subject to a specified minimum limit. The amount to set as a minimum limit will depend upon the work to be performed by the contractor. There may also be additional coverages that should be requested. The organization's agent or broker should assist in determining appropriate insurance requirements to use in contracts.

4

Umbrella Liability Insurance

After World War II, Lloyds of London developed a special policy for business organizations that had ocean-related liability risks, often referred to as wet marine or blue water marine. These policies were referred to as bumbershoots and provided substantially higher policy limits over the limits normally provided by primary markets. In addition, substantially broader coverage was usually provided.

In the late 1950s, Lloyds and American insurance companies began offering specific excess policies for land-related liability risks. To differentiate these policies from the marine-related policies, the term *umbrella* became popular. Again, these policies were often much broader than the primary policies written by traditional insurance companies.

Coverage

Figure 4.1 gives an example of the various functions of an umbrella policy. The umbrella provides first-dollar coverage over the limits of the primary policy, which usually range in the area of $300,000 to $500,000. In those areas where the umbrella provides broader coverage, coverage would drop down to a self-insured retention of $10,000 or $25,000. Stated another way, the insured would be required to pay the first $10,000 or $25,000 and then the umbrella would pay amounts in excess of this self-insured retention.

The application of the umbrella policy is fairly simple. Let's assume that the primary policy provides a $500,000 limit while the umbrella provides a $1 million limit. Let's further assume an automobile loss

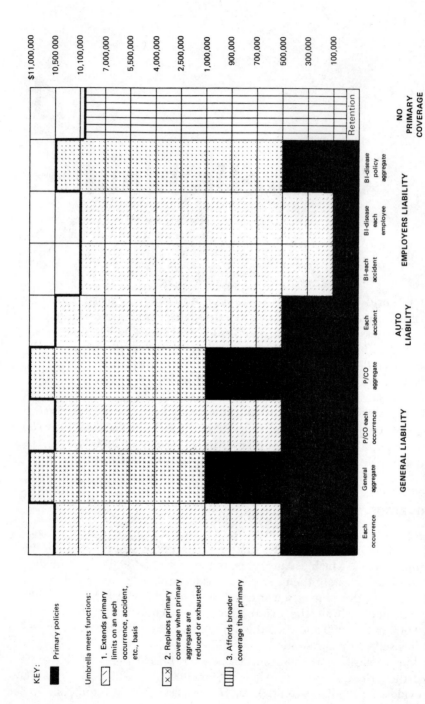

Figure 4.1. Functions of a $10 million umbrella policy. (*Source: Reprinted from Commercial Liability Insurance with permission of the publisher, International Risk Management Institute, Inc. Copyright © 1986.*)

involving an ultimate claim of $1 million. The primary policy would exhaust its per occurrence limit by paying $500,000 and then the umbrella would pay the $500,000 of loss in excess of the first $500,000. On the other hand, if the primary policy did not cover the incident, the insured would be responsible for the first $25,000 (a self-insured retention) and the umbrella policy would pay the next $975,000.

In the 1960s, this became a very popular policy; by 1975, virtually every business organization of any size carried an umbrella of at least $1 million. As a result, an entirely new specialty market developed to provide these policies. Unlike the standard commercial general liability policy, there is no standard wording. Coverage and cost are entirely negotiable in most states.

As the premium volume of these specialty markets grew over the years, the traditional insurance companies providing the primary policies began to develop their own umbrella programs, which were usually written in connection with their primary policies to take advantage of the developing market.

In summary, the primary function of umbrella policies is to provide high limits of liability above general, auto, and employers liability insurance for catastrophic losses. They also usually "drop down" to become first dollar insurance if the aggregate limits of these primary policies are exhausted because of loss frequency.

Ways to Reduce Costs

This chapter presents eight ways to reduce umbrella liability costs.

38. Consider Alternative Primary Limits

As the insurance market progresses through its cycles, the umbrella and primary insurance markets develop ever-changing attitudes to the *intermediate risk layer*, which might be defined as that layer between $300,000 and $1 million. For instance, during a buyer's market, when pricing is soft, the umbrella markets will normally develop an aggressive pricing posture for this risk layer as compared to the primary markets. As a result, a general rule is that umbrella markets will be more competitive in this risk layer than the standard, well-known primary markets.

On the other hand, as the market evolves into a tight, seller's market, the umbrella markets will pull back and provide coverage only in excess of higher underlying limits. While some of the umbrella markets may agree to provide the intermediate layer, the pricing will normally be substantially higher than the primary markets. At the same time, the primary markets normally pursue a more stable pricing approach and their pricing will be much more competitive than the umbrella markets.

Therefore, the preferred approach is to obtain quotes for alternative primary limits from the primary carrier, as well as for varying attachment points from the umbrella markets, to see which market segment will be more competitive in the intermediate risk layer.

In summary, primary markets will be more competitive in an intermediate risk layer during tight markets while the umbrella markets will be more competitive during soft markets.

39. Obtain Quotes for Buffer Layers

The intermediate risk layer is often described as a buffer layer. For a brief period during the transitional periods of the market, the buyer should obtain quotes for this buffer layer from a third market. If a buffer layer is purchased, Figure 4.2 indicates the resulting insurance program.

When neither the primary nor the umbrella markets want to be involved in the buffer layer and, as a result, both are charging substantially higher premiums, it may be better to determine the limits and attachment points at which both will become most comfortable and competitive. Since the specialty market will want to attach at a higher level and the primary will want to provide lower limits, a third market must be used to provide the buffer layer. For example, a buffer layer might be used to fill the gap between $300,000 and $500,000 or between $500,000 and $1 million. Usually, the premiums for this buffer layer will border upon being exorbitant. However, the premiums saved by removing pressure from the primary and specialty markets may far exceed the additional cost of the buffer layer.

Again, depending on the volatility of the market, the buffer window may be open for only 3 to 6 months during a transitional period of the marketplace.

40. Get Competitive Pricing

To say that the umbrella market is volatile is a gross understatement. Umbrella markets come and go almost as quickly as other markets change their pricing philosophy. In addition, markets' attitudes for certain risk categories, such as contractors, oil risks, and manufacturers,

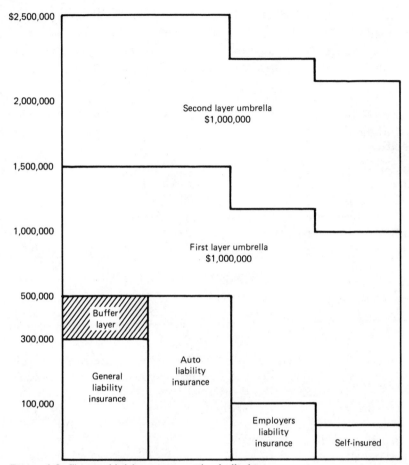

Figure 4.2. Illustrated liability program with a buffer layer.

will change as underwriters move from one company to the other. Therefore, it is extremely important that all the potential markets for your risk be contacted.

However, extreme care should be taken in approaching the overall marketplace. It is usually preferable to use one insurance agent to contact all of the specialty markets since these markets work on a "brokerage" basis and will work with any financially viable insurance agent or broker. On the other hand, no one agent represents all the primary companies that will write umbrellas only over their own primary policies. Therefore, it may be advisable to do some market research to determine which primary companies are competitive in your geographical area and type of business and to contact one or two other agents who have access to these markets and who are generally regarded as profitable and desirable agents by those markets.

At the same time, loyalty usually pays off in the insurance business. Therefore, if your umbrella carrier is still actively seeking umbrella business, special emphasis should be placed on approaching that particular market.

41. Submit Well-Prepared Specifications

It is amazing how similar bank officers and insurance company underwriters are. Since most organizations deal with banks directly, they are more familiar with making presentations to banks. For instance, two organizations approach a bank for a line of credit. One delivers a very polished presentation concerning its financial position, its business opportunities, and its risks. It will probably receive better terms than the other business organization, which walks in with a handwritten yellow sheet of paper, intending to simply promise to pay back the money at some indefinite point in the future.

The same careful approach should be taken with insurance underwriters. It is highly desirable that the insurance market be approached with well-prepared insurance specifications which outline the operations and risks of the prospective insured. If the premiums are large enough, consideration should be given to having the chief financial officer or president of the insured make a personal presentation to the underwriters who are most likely to offer the best proposal. In many cases, this personal approach saves thousands of premium dollars and obtains important coverages.

While the insured may have the capabilities of preparing the submission, they are usually prepared by the insurance agent or broker. Either way, the business manager should demand an opportunity to review the submission before it is given to underwriters. This puts pressure on the agent or broker to do a superior job. Also, the business manager should verify the accuracy of the data provided and make suggestions to improve it. Time spent in this area pays great dividends.

42. Determine the Premium Basis

The umbrella premiums are generally determined by applying a percentage to the premiums charged by the primary carrier for the underlying limits. During a tight insurance market, umbrella underwriters often use manual premiums before any discounts to apply their rating percentages to develop the umbrella premium. Since these umbrella underwriters may not be entirely familiar with your business operations, erroneous manual premiums may be developed through the use of improper classifications. Therefore, it is usually desirable for the business manager and/or the agent to develop the estimated manual premiums based on proper and correct rating classifications.

In the vast majority of instances, umbrella underwriters apply their rating percentages to the actual premium to be charged by the primary carrier. For instance, in a soft market the first $1 million of umbrella coverage will range between 9 and 12 percent of the primary premium; but during a tighter market, the percentage will range from 17.5 to 27.5 percent. At the same time, the premiums charged by the primary carrier will increase or decrease based on the market. This results in a great deal of volatility in umbrella premiums.

Generally, the $4 million layer above $1 million will be at approximately the same cost as the first $1 million while $5 million excess $5 million will be 40 to 60 percent of the premium paid for the $5 million underlying umbrella limit.

Therefore, it is critical for the insured to negotiate the very best price possible for the auto and general liability primary premiums. In addition, reasonable deductibles of $250 to $1,000 might be assumed to further depress premiums. If dividends or retrospective rating returns are expected, then the estimated premium should be reduced accordingly.

If the primary carrier is underwriting the account on a package basis—including workers compensation, property coverage, and inland marine coverages, for example—then premiums for these other lines might be increased and the auto/general liability premiums reduced by the same amount. The primary underwriter will be getting the same overall premium, while the insured may be charged a somewhat lower umbrella premium.

In a soft, buyer's insurance market, primary liability *and* umbrella liability premiums can often be reduced by purchasing lower primary limits (e.g., $500,000 instead of $1 million). The primary insurers charge less because they are providing lower limits. The umbrella insurer should charge more, because of the lower attachment point, but actually charges less when the umbrella premium is determined by applying a flat percentage to the primary premiums. This approach does not work in a tight market because umbrella carriers refuse to drop down over lower primary limits. Based on the above percentages, for every dollar saved in the general liability/auto liability area, another $.50 may be saved assuming a $5 million umbrella is purchased.

43. Select Reasonable Umbrella Limits

It is surprising how few umbrella claims are actually paid. Those that are paid normally involve large businesses. However, when suits are filed, the damages requested are far in excess of actual damages. As a result, without higher limits the insured will become fearful of a possible settlement over its limits while financial institutions providing credit may become concerned and may begin reducing available credit.

Therein lies a very difficult question. What limits of coverage should the business organization carry? You cannot expect your insurance agent to give you a concrete answer. Agents have their own errors and omissions liability insurance to worry about. The thought will occur to them that if they recommend that you drop your limits from $5 million to $1 million, the next day one of your employees may be involved in an automobile accident with a carload of highly paid surgeons on the way to a medical convention. As a result, agents have a tendency to play it safe and recommend higher limits. As usual, the buck stops with the president of your organization.

Table 4.1 is a sample of limits suggested by some insurance professionals. Note its suggestion that all organizations should purchase at least a $1 million umbrella over the primary policies. Many insurance professionals think that $5 million should be the absolute minimum for any organization. Obviously, the nature of operations must be taken into consideration. For instance, a petrochemical plant operating close to a populated area needs higher limits than a small manufacturer of relatively safe products located in a small town.

In some cases, customers will dictate the limits required. Often, these required limits, reflecting an insurance market that has changed, will be excessive. If so, simply asking the customer to reduce the requirements in view of the current market conditions may result in a desired reduction, thereby making the organization more competitive and saving the customer unnecessary costs.

Table 4.1 Rules of Thumb for Umbrella Liability Coverage Limits (In thousands)

Sales	Limits
Under 2,000	1,000
2–5,000	2,000
5–10,000	3,000
10–15,000	4,000
15–25,000	5,000
25–50,000	10,000
50–100.000	15,000
100–250,000	20–25,000
250–500,000	25–50,000
500,000–1,000,000	50–100,000
Over 1,000,000	Subject to availability

In any event, reducing limits can be a gut-wrenching decision; but it is important in containing umbrella costs during tight markets.

44. Provide for Automatic Extensions

During soft markets, plenty of umbrella capacity can be found at extremely low pricing. Just about the time that the average purchaser of insurance comes to expect this approach, the market changes and capacity dries up while prices go through the roof. This becomes very frustrating to the average buyer of insurance, who often becomes hostile in the process.

In soft markets, most insurance companies will have cut back on personnel to contain costs. When the market turns, most insureds and agents begin contacting a greater number of markets with greater frequency. This, in turn, overloads the system that underwriters have maintained in producing quotations and, as a result, quotations— particularly from the better markets—may not be received by the agents and their customers until a week before renewal. In some cases, it may only be the day before renewal. Usually, the closer to expiration that the insured receives a quote, the worse it will be. Therefore, all types of subtle and not so subtle pressure should be exerted to get quotes in earlier rather than later. With all the best intentions and efforts, however, this may not happen.

Many insureds will negotiate an agreement to provide automatic extensions during the competitive phase of the market. For instance, the existing insurance company agrees ahead of time that if it does not provide a renewal quote within 30 days of expiration, it will automatically extend the existing policy for 30 or 60 days beyond the expiration date at the same terms, conditions, and cost. Therefore, if a shocking quote is received a week or day before renewal, the buyer has time to reenter the market and try to find a better quotation.

This same approach is desirable for other major coverages such as general and auto liability policies. Again, this agreement will be available only in a buyer's market, but it will help avoid surprises and the need to make last-minute decisions regarding the first renewal that takes place after the market tightens.

45. Use Care with Adjustable Rate Policies

Some underwriters will quote premiums that are "flat." These nonadjustable premiums apply whether the business grows or decreases in size.

In other words, the premium is not inflation sensitive. If a new company is formed or acquired, however, a pro rata charge may be made. In softer markets, flat premiums are usually used as a competitive tool, especially if the economy is in an upswing which will result in a greater volume of business for the insured. Therefore, as a general statement, during soft markets it is more desirable to seek flat premiums based on conservative estimates of business volume.

On the other hand, during a tight market, underwriters will favor adjustable rate policies which are based on rates per $100 of payroll, receipts, mileage, or possibly hours worked. If the company is growing, these policies can result in some very undesirable surprises at the end of the policy term when the insurance company asks for a substantial additional premium after auditing the insured's books. Alternatively, adjustable rate umbrella policies are usually subject to a *minimum premium*, which allows the insurer to avoid returning significant amounts of premium if the business contracts.

Generally, the larger the business organization, the lower the composite rate per unit. Perhaps the best approach is to supply an optimistic estimate of the business volume, which should result in a lower rate per unit. At the same time, however, a high minimum premium based on the higher estimated volume should be avoided. Preferably, the minimum premium should be 50 to 75 percent of the premium that would be incurred at the estimated business volume.

The unit to which the rate will be applied can be very important. For instance, in times of inflationary pressures, it is desirable to avoid the use of receipts or payroll. The more desirable approach would be hours worked for contractors, mileage for trucking companies, number of employees for service firms, or manufactured units for manufacturers. A similar approach might be taken with the underlying auto and general liability policies as well.

5
Workers Compensation

At the beginning of this century, the United States was emerging as an industrialized nation and society was also developing a social conscience. At that point in time, employees who were injured on the job had to sue their employer under common law to obtain benefits. Employers had basic common law defenses which were very difficult to overcome in court. Since average employees had very little if any savings, it was virtually impossible for them to hire an attorney to represent their interest. As a result, injured employees and their families often ended up in the poorhouse.

Beginning in 1911 with Wisconsin, each state began to pass workers compensation statutes which amounted to a tradeoff between the employer and the employee. Under these statutes, the employers agreed to give up their common law defenses and, in return, received limited liability as respects weekly indemnity and medical benefits. Employees gained by receiving "no fault" benefits if injured on the job. Each state individually passed its own workers compensation statute and, in 1927, the Congress passed the U.S. Longshore and Harbor Workers' Compensation Act providing benefits to longshoremen, who were not considered covered under the individual states' statutes.

Benefits provided to employees are covered by the standard workers compensation policy in most states. Today's workers compensation policy has three basic coverage parts.

Part One provides coverage for the statutory liability of the employer under the specified state statutes. Rather than insuring a specific individual or a class of individuals, the employer insures the liability created by state statutes. However, some employees—such as domestic help and agricultural employees—as well as sole proprietors/partners are often excluded under the law and have to be specifically added to the policy for coverage to apply.

Part Two provides coverage for any liability that the employee decides to present to the employer under common law. This applies in those few situations where the employee can elect not to come under the workers compensation statute. In most states, if the employee decides to press a common law liability suit, benefits under Part One are forfeited.

Part Three provides for statutory benefits when employees can press claims in states other than those where they are working. This *other states coverage* may come into play when, for example, an employee is injured while traveling in a state that provides higher benefits than the state in which he or she normally works. This coverage should be structured to apply to all states except those specified in Part One and the monopolistic fund states listed below.

It is interesting to note that the United States is the only major industrialized nation that has a private workers compensation system. In most countries, workers compensation is part of a social security program. However, there are six U.S. states which do not allow the private insurance industry to fund benefits. Instead, monopolistic state funds have been established by the states of Nevada, North Dakota, Ohio, Washington, West Virginia, and Wyoming. If the employer has operations in these states, a policy must be purchased from the monopolistic state fund.

In Arizona, California, Colorado, Idaho, Maryland, Michigan, Minnesota, Montana, New York, Oklahoma, Pennsylvania, and Utah, competitive state funds compete in the open marketplace with private industry.

If the employer is a stevedore or has employees working on stationary platforms—such as oil rigs located over navigable bodies of water—the employer may be subject to the U.S. Longshore and Harbor Workers' Compensation Act, which allows substantially higher benefits than most state acts. A specific endorsement is required to provide this coverage under the standard policy.

For the average business, the workers compensation premium is the largest single property and casualty insurance premium paid. Arranging proper coverage is not especially difficult, but obtaining the most efficient program from a cost standpoint can be very difficult due to the various factors involved.

Ways to Control Costs

This chapter covers four important ways to control workers compensation costs. Chapters 6 and 10, which also provide ways to control workers compensation insurance costs, should be reviewed along with this chapter.

46. Get Correct Classifications

The first step toward controlling workers compensation cost is to be sure that your payrolls are being properly classified. To rate workers compensation insurance, the insurance industry uses classification codes that are similar to the SIC codes developed by the government. Figure 5.1, a page from the workers compensation classification table, is an example. Each classification code has its own corresponding rate that is multiplied

CARPENTRY — DETACHED one or two family
DWELLINGS 5645

    Includes garages constructed in connection with the dwellings.

CARPENTRY — DWELLINGS — THREE STORIES
OR LESS... 5651

    Applicable only to buildings designed primarily for multiple dwelling occupancy and includes garages constructed in connection therewith. Carpentry in the the construction of detached private dwellings for occupancy by one or two families to be separately rated as 5645 carpentry.

CARPENTRY — INSTALLATION of CABINET
WORK or INTERIOR TRIM 5437

    Not applicable to contractors who perform any other carpentry operations at the same job or location.

CARPENTRY — INSTALLATION of FINISHED
WOODEN FLOORING 5437

    Includes installation of parquet flooring. Not applicable to contractors who perform any other carpentry operations at the same job or location.

CARPENTRY—SHOP ONLY—& Drivers 2802

    Codes 2802 and 2731 planing or molding mill shall not be assigned to the same risk unless the operations described by these classifications are conducted as separate and distinct businesses. Commercial lumber yards, building materials dealers or fuel and material dealers to be separately rated. Where a risk deals in any lumber or building materials or in any fuel and materials in addition to performing carpentry shop operations, all yard operations, including all drivers, shall be rated in the appropriate yard classification, 8232.

CARPENTRY NOC... 5403

★ CARPET, Rug or Upholstery CLEANING—shop or
  outside & Drivers 2585

CARPET or Rug MFG—JUTE OR HEMP 2220

CARPET or Rug MFG NOC 2402

CARRIAGE or Wagon MFG OR ASSEMBLY 3808

    Baby carriage mfg. to be separately rated as 3865.

CARRIER SYSTEM — PNEUMATIC — INSTALLA-
TION OR REPAIR & Drivers 5183

    Applies to work inside of buildings. Installation of freight carrier systems rated as 3724 millwright work.

CARTRIDGE MFG OR LOADING—
See "EXPLOSIVES"

CASH REGISTER MFG... 3574

CASKET or Coffin MFG OR ASSEMBLY—METAL 3076

CASKET or Coffin MFG OR ASSEMBLY—WOOD 2881

    Includes the mfg. of metal fittings.

CASKET or Coffin UPHOLSTERING and Burial
Garment Mfg 9522

CATERER 9079

CATHEDRAL or Art Glass WINDOW MFG 4133

    Includes glass mfg.

CATTLE DEALER & Salespersons, Drivers.............. 8288

    Not operating farms or ranches.

CEILING INSTALLATION—SUSPENDED ACOUS-
TICAL GRID TYPE 5020

    Insulation work separately rated.

CEMENT MFG... 1701

    Excavation or digging, dredging, mining or quarrying to be separately rated.

CEMETERY OPERATION & Drivers.......................... 9220

CHAIN MFG—FORGED 3110

CHARCOAL MFG & Drivers 1472

    Includes distillation.

CHARITABLE or Religious ORGANIZATION —
welfare—ALL OPERATIONS & Drivers 8837

    Includes stores and collecting, conditioning and resale of used donated articles of the household type.

CHAUFFEURS & Helpers NOC—commercial 7380

    Subject to the Standard Exception Manual Rule.

Figure 5.1 . Illustrative workers compensation classifications. (*Source: Used with permission of The National Council on Compensation Insurance.*)

by the payroll associated with the operations included in the code. Of course, insurance buyers will want to use the code(s) with the lowest rate(s) and the insurance underwriter will opt for the code(s) with the highest rates. While some operations are easy to classify because there is only one "governing code" (e.g., playing card manufacturers), others are very difficult because numerous codes are possibly applicable. For example, over 60 classifications might apply to construction operations. The various classifications are arranged in over 130 groups of industry classifications.

Development of Rates.   While the workers compensation classification system has been standardized in most states, monopolistic states have their own classification systems, and a few nonmonopolistic states such as California, New Jersey, and Pennsylvania also have their own classification systems. The system that applies nationally is administered by the National Council on Compensation Insurance (NCCI). The states that do not use the NCCI system have their own bureaus.

The various rating jurisdictions collect statistics for each classification, such as payrolls and losses to develop *pure loss rates* for each type of activity. Added to these pure loss rates are nonloss expenses such as premium taxes, agent's commissions, insurance company overhead, and other similar expenses to develop the *manual rate*. These manual rates are listed in the applicable workers compensation rating manuals.

Review Current Classification(s) and Look for Alternatives.   The first step in determining (or confirming) the proper classification(s) for your particular business is to sit down with your insurance agent, consultant, or insurance company representative—with the workers compensation manual—and develop a list of all classifications that might apply to your particular business. At the same time, look up the manual rates for each classification in each state where you do business.

The current classification approach should then be reviewed to see if any new classifications might be applied or if some classifications are being used erroneously. Often, there will be gray areas, which can be negotiated with the insurance company; or perhaps a favorable ruling can be requested from the applicable rating bureau. Again, an insurance professional can be of great help in this process.

If certain of your operations can be reclassified to effect lower premium costs, a meeting should be scheduled with the insurance company to obtain its concurrence. If the insurance company disagrees, and you feel that you have a good case, you may request an inspection by the bureau having jurisdiction to make a ruling. If the insurance company disagrees, this does not mean that its representatives are being unduly arbitrary. It simply reflects the many gray areas in payroll classification and the fact that reasonable disagreements can arise.

In any event, after the appropriate classification procedures are developed, they should be confirmed in writing and, preferably, put into a simple workbook to be followed by accounting personnel. Many classification errors occur after a turnover of employees. The trained employee leaves, and the replacement begins to misclassify the payrolls.

If you discover a gross misclassification in your favor, many states will allow the insured to recover past overcharges subject to the statute of limitations for written contracts in that particular state.

Preferably, the classification process should not be approached in an adversarial manner. Careful communication with your insurance underwriter and insurance company auditor, assisted by your insurance agent or consultant, normally will produce the best possible results.

Workers Compensation Manuals. Workers compensation insurance is one of the most codified areas of property and casualty insurance. The NCCI issues a *Basic Manual for Workers Compensation and Employers Liability Insurance* that includes rules, regulations, and rates for most states. The other states publish their own manuals. All of these manuals explain in great detail how payrolls should be classified and give rules concerning the division of certain payrolls. In some instances, if a number of people work in the same room, performing various tasks, all of the employees must be classified under the highest rated classification. On the other hand, some classes, such as construction, will allow a division of payroll. There are also rules as to how certain payrolls—such as overtime—can be excluded and how payrolls of owners and partners and other exempt employees might be treated. Since workers compensation is the most expensive policy for many businesses, it behooves the average business manager to read the more important rules and regulations. Fortunately, they are not very lengthy. The applicable manual(s) might be borrowed from an insurance agent or consultant or, if continued use is contemplated, a personal copy can be ordered from the NCCI at the following address:

National Council on Compensation Insurance
750 Park of Commerce Drive
Boca Raton, FL 33431

In addition, the NCCI has licensed International Risk Management Institute, Inc. (IRMI), to reprint certain portions of its manual. The IRMI manual goes a step further by elaborating on the application of the rules, regulations, and classifications. State rate updates are also available. This manual can be ordered from:

International Risk Management Institute
12222 Merit Drive
Suite 1660
Dallas, Texas 75251

Unless the buyer is armed with an up-to-date copy of the applicable workers compensation manual, proper classification of payroll may be very difficult.

47. Delete Overtime Payroll Surcharge

All states, with the exception of Delaware and Pennsylvania, allow for the deletion of the premium portion of overtime in developing payrolls used in rating workers compensation insurance. For instance, if the hourly wage rate is $10, an employee will be paid this rate for the first 40 hours; for each hour thereafter, a 50 percent premium will apply. In other words, an hourly rate of $15 will be paid.

From a workers compensation risk standpoint, there is no greater risk at the 41st hour than at the 1st hour of work during that particular week. Therefore, for insurance purposes, if the employee works 50 hours, the 50 hours are multiplied by the $10 hourly rate and, in turn, the employer reports $500 of ratable payroll to the insurance company. The overtime premium of $50 (10 hours × $5) is deleted from the rating base.

If the insured fails to maintain books as respects this overtime premium, substantial overcharges may occur.

48. Use a "First-Aid" Folder

The majority of workers compensation claims involve "medical only" claims. These are instances where an employee suffers a minor injury and is taken to an industrial clinic or emergency room. While medical treatment may continue, very little time loss is sustained. If these claims are reported to the insurance company with a request for payment, the doctor will be required to complete lengthy insurance forms, as well as submitting individual bills. In addition, it will be necessary for the insurance company to process the claim.

As a result, the doctor may add as much as 50 percent to the medical bill for processing the claim, while the insurance company may incur as much as $50 in processing the payment. In the long run, this expense is charged back to the employer through insurance experience rating or reduced dividends.

Many employers can establish an arrangement with their insurance carrier whereby small medical only claims up to a predetermined amount of approximately $200 to $250 will be paid directly by the employer, unless the employer requests otherwise on a specific claim.

The employer makes an arrangement with one or more clinics to treat injured employees. These clinics are requested to submit monthly billings to the employer for all services rendered. The employer continues to complete injury reports and will usually file these with the insurance company with the notation that, "This report is for information purposes only." Therefore, the doctors will not charge for their paperwork and the administrative cost of the insurance company will be avoided. On the other hand, if a claim develops and is more serious than originally thought, then the insurance company can be requested to activate a file.

This approach is only practical when there are a sufficient number of claims at a particular location to justify it. In Illinois, the statute allows the employer to assume the first $1,000 of medical expense, whether it involves a lost time claim or not. In return, an attractive credit is applied to premiums. This approach may be adopted by other states in the future.

49. Take Advantage of Dividends and Flexible Rates

Prior to 10 years ago, virtually all states required all insurance companies to use the same rates for specific industry classifications. In recent years, some states began allowing insurance companies to use insurance rates based on their own experience to encourage more competition. Other states required use of the same base rates but allowed insurance companies to apply credits or surcharges to these standard rates. Figure 5.2 shows the states in which *open rating* or *schedule credits/debits* are allowed. During the "buyer's market" of the early 1980s, workers compensation rates were heavily discounted. During the tight insurance market which developed during the period of 1984 to 1987, buyers were often subjected to higher rates filed by insurance companies or to surcharge rates.

In the states where flexible rating or schedule credits are unavailable, dividend plans may be used to adjust rates. These dividend plans typically fall into three categories: (1) flat dividends, (2) retention plans, (3) sliding-scale plans.

	Effective date	*Schedule rating*	*Open rating*
Alabama	9/1/82	±15%	
Arizona	7/1/82	±25%	
Arkansas	6/17/81		x
Colorado			x
Delaware	9/10/82	±25%	
District of Columbia	2/1/83	±25%	
Georgia	1/1/84		x
Illinois	1/1/83		x
Kentucky	7/15/82		x
Maine	1/1/86		x
Michigan	1/1/83		x
Minnesota	1/1/84		x
Mississippi	11/1/83	±25%	
Missouri	11/11/83	±15%	
New Mexico	5/1/82	±15%	
Oregon	7/18/2		x
Rhode Island	9/1/82		x
South Carolina	2/1/83	±25%	
South Dakota	10/1/82	±25%	
Tennessee	5/1/83	±25%	
Utah	1/1/83	±25%	
Vermont	7/1/84		x

Figure 5.2. States that allow schedule rating or open rating of workers compensation insurance.

A *flat dividend* is usually paid regardless of the insured's loss experience. However, it should be realized that underwriters will not agree to place an insured with poor past loss experience in a dividend plan. Dividends will range between 6 and 9 percent.

A *retention plan* is more of a cost-plus program. The insurance company develops a cost factor, called a retention factor, based on its operating expenses, reinsurance premiums, agents' commissions, premium taxes, and loss-handling fees. The remaining funds are used to pay losses, with any surplus returned to the insured at the end of the year as a dividend. For example, let's assume that all of these expenses amount to a percentage factor of 30 percent of the premium. Let's further assume that the insured sustains losses equal to 50 percent of the premium.Therefore, the insurance company will retain 30 percent of the premium for expenses and 50 percent for losses; it will return the balance of 20 percent to the insured in the form of a dividend about 12 to 24 months after expiration of the insurance policy.

A *sliding-scale* dividend plan is similar, in that it is based upon losses. However, the insurance company will use a table which indicates a percentage of return based on the loss ratio (losses divided by premiums). For instance, if the insured has a 25 percent loss ratio, a return of 20 percent might be paid. On the other hand, if the loss ratio was higher, say 50 percent, the dividend paid might be approximately 13 percent.

Generally speaking, retention plans will return more money at low loss ratios, while the sliding-scale plan will allow more returns at higher loss ratios.

Overall, dividend plans are to reward insureds for controlling losses, as well as allowing the insurance company some flexibility in adjusting the premium rates to reflect its individual operating expenses and investment programs.

An important caveat to the buyer is that dividends are not guaranteed. In fact, most states have laws which prohibit such guarantees. Therefore, though an insured may earn a dividend, if the insurance company's board of directors decides not to declare dividends, no such dividend will be forthcoming.

In summary, open rating, schedule credits/debits, and dividends have an important impact on the net cost of workers compensation insurance. Therefore, the buyer should know how these programs work and what is available from the insurance industry.

6
Experience Rating

Although Louisiana and Texas also have state-supervised experience rating plans for general liability and auto liability, this chapter will deal with experience rating of workers compensation, which is applicable in virtually every state. The National Council on Compensation Insurance (NCCI) administers a master experience rating plan that is applicable in most states. However, there are a number of experience rating plans which apply to the individual states. In "monopolistic" states, only the state itself is authorized to provide workers compensation coverage, and each of these six states develops its own individual experience rating plan. Other states—such as California, Louisiana, and Texas—have their own individual experience rating plans which apply if all of the insured's operations are within those particular states.

In all instances, the purpose of experience rating plans is to have the premium charged for coverage reflect the experience of individual policyholders. For instance, if the prescribed formula develops a 20 percent credit, then the insured will pay 80 percent of the applicable manual rates. On the other hand, if the insured has had poor loss experience, and develops a modifier of 1.20 or a 20 percent debit, the applicable standard rates are surcharged by 20 percent. Assuming no major shifts in payroll, the credits applied to all policies written should equal the debits applied so that the insurance industry, as a whole, obtains premiums based on payrolls times the standard rates. The purpose of this system of credits and debits is to encourage safety practices by rewarding employers who control their losses, while penalizing employers who have adverse loss experience.

Experience Rating Overview

Unfortunately, most insurance buyers and many insurance agents do not thoroughly understand how the experience rating process works. To effectively control insurance costs, it is very important that the development of experience modifiers be closely monitored by both insurance buyers and agents/brokers.

To calculate an experience modifier, the individual loss experience of an individual insured is compared to the expected experience of the insured's industry group. It is important to note that modifiers are not a function of loss ratios, i.e., past losses divided by past premiums. Instead, current expected loss rates are multiplied by past payrolls and compared to past losses. Therefore, as long as an employer can maintain low losses, substantial credits can be earned.

One of the most basic experience rating concepts to understand is that the experience rating formula penalizes insureds that have a *high frequency* of losses more than it does insureds that have a *high severity* of losses. In other words, an insured with $100,000 in past workers compensation losses will have a higher modifier if there were 100 losses of $1,000 each than if there were 10 losses of $10,000 each. The rationale for this is that it is easier to reduce the number of on-the-job accidents than it is to reduce the severity of the injuries that result from the accidents that do occur. Therefore, an insured that is implementing a safety program for the first time should focus first on techniques that will reduce the number of on-the-job accidents.

The experience period used in developing experience modifiers is 3 years, but the most current year is not counted. Let's assume that the workers compensation policy will renew on October 1, 1987. The policy years to be used begin October 1, 1985, 1984, and 1983. The latest year, which began on October 1, 1986, and ended on September 30, 1987, will not be used because the expiring policy has not been audited to determine exact payrolls by classification. In addition, some of the losses to be covered by the 1987 policy will probably not be reported until 3 to 6 months after policy expiration. Therefore, the 3 "mature" years which ended just prior to the expiring policy period are used.

Ways to Control Costs

This chapter covers six ways to control workers compensation costs by understanding experience rating.

50. Review Reserves

Each insurance company, one or more, involved during the 3-year experience period to be used is required to report payrolls and initial losses and loss reserves for the latest year. On the older 2d and 3d years, insurance companies report any changes in claims and claim reserves since the last modifier was calculated. It is important to note that reserves for unpaid claims are used and count as if they have been paid. These losses are to be "valued" 6 months after the end of the policy period. Therefore, for an October 1 renewal, the valuation date used to compute the experience modifier is April 1.

It is desirable for the insured to negotiate an arrangement whereby the insured can review reserves before they are reported to the NCCI. The usual procedure is to meet with the claims manager of the insurance company just prior to the 6-month evaluation. The insurance company should prepare an analysis of open claims. These outstanding claims are reviewed with the insured and the reserved amounts are evaluated and adjusted, based on the common consensus. In some cases, eventual outcome of many cases may be known; but due to the fact that it takes 90 days for paperwork to wind its way through the insurance company, the reserve may not have been adjusted. Shortly after the review, the insurance company can speed up the process so that the actual filings with the NCCI will reflect the most current status of the claims.

51. Prepare a Test Modifier

After the claims have been reviewed, the insurance agent or insurance company should prepare a "test rating" for the policyholder. This will allow the policyholder to budget its estimated insurance cost for the 12-month period beginning approximately 5 months hence. Just as important, it allows the policyholder and its advisors to develop a renewal strategy. For instance, if the experience modifier is expected to drop substantially, the policyholder may be advised to assume a guaranteed cost program with a flat dividend. On the other hand, if there is going to be an increase in the modifier, especially in the debit range, the policyholder should work on improving its safety program, as well as giving serious thought to assuming a more aggressive cost-plus plan, such as a dividend retention plan or a retrospective rating plan.

The bottom line is that an insured cannot purchase workers compensation intelligently without forecasting the experience rating modifier.

52. Review Final Modifier

Theoretically, the official modifier should be promulgated and issued by the appropriate board or bureau within 6 weeks prior to the anniversary date. Unfortunately, this is not usually the case because rate changes may be pending, insurance companies involved in the experience period may not have filed their information in a timely manner, or—in some cases—the rating organization is simply behind in its paperwork. This, again, underscores the importance of test ratings.

Usually, the official modifier will be received within 90 days after the expiration date. When it is published, the insured should obtain a copy of the work sheet showing the calculation. Obviously, if the official modifier is the same as the test modifier, no further action is indicated. However, if there is a difference between the two, additional action is indicated. Payrolls should be checked, losses in the test rating should be compared to those in the promulgated rating, and so forth.

One reason for a difference could simply be the fact that rates changed during the period between the test rating and the official rating. Rating factors used in the experience rating process invariably change at the time of a manual rate change.

However, it is also possible that the bureau made errors in calculating the modifier. Payrolls may have been left out, some other employer's experience may have been included, or a number of other clerical errors may have been made. When such errors or mistakes are pointed out, the applicable rating bureaus are usually very cooperative in recalculating the modifier.

53. Check Payroll and Losses Used

Experience modifiers are calculated by rating bureaus. Each insured employer has a risk identification number. In the process of keypunching information, it is possible for the data entry clerk to simply transpose two numbers, so that you lose some of your experience, or to include another firm's experience in your calculation. There have even been instances in which payrolls for an entire year have been omitted. If losses are included without the payroll to offset such losses, there is a substantial negative effect on the experience modifier.

To summarize, actual payrolls and losses should be checked during the test rating process and then payrolls and losses used in the test rating should be compared to the official data.

54. Understand Acquisition, Merger, and Spin-Off Implications

All entities which have a common ownership interest of more than 50 percent should be combined for experience rating purposes. This is even the case if, for example, one of the entities is a trucking company, another is a contractor, and the third is a hardware store. The workers compensation manuals discussed in Chapter 5 outline the rules that apply to a combination of entities. However, these entities will not be combined unless the governing boards and bureaus are notified. As a result, many businesses that should be combined for experience rating purposes are not.

In some cases, it will be to the benefit of the insureds to have their data combined. For instance, the larger the overall exposure basis, the larger the credits that can be developed. Therefore, if all combinable entities have not been combined, a test rating should be prepared, combining all entities to see the overall net effect on the insurance costs for all entities. Since the modifiers for all of the entities become averaged, the entity with the best loss ratio ends up having a higher modifier under the combined approach, while the entity with the worst loss ratio has a lower modifier than it would develop on its own. This inequity can be dealt with internally by simply weighting the modifiers. For example, the entity with the best experience would have a lower assigned modifier than the entity with the worst loss ratio. However, the overall premiums developed for the overall operation would still be those required by the insurance company in applying the overall average modifier. At the same time, the organization as a whole would still have a lower modifier than was applicable before the combination.

On the negative side, the larger the exposure base, the more self-rated is the overall group. Therefore, with individual experience rating plans, larger losses may have been heavily discounted. When combined, much of this discounting may be dropped, thereby causing an overall higher premium with the average modifier, as compared to the premium before the combination.

Discontinued Operations.   From time to time, corporations discontinue operations of a subsidiary which has lost money. The problems causing the economic losses may also have caused substantial workers compensation losses. Unfortunately, if no action is taken, the bad losses from these discontinued operations continue in the experience rating plan of the ongoing business enterprise. It may be possible to sell the shell company prior to discontinuing the operations, often to a nominee person such as a lawyer, in such a manner as to transfer the experience out of the current experience rating plan. For instance, $\frac{1}{3}$ can be sold one day, $\frac{1}{3}$ the next day, and $\frac{1}{3}$ the next day. Forms can then be filed with the rating bureau, establishing that separate ownership has occurred with that particular corporation, and the experience can be deleted from the parent company's calculation.

Mergers and Acquisitions. When new companies are formed and acquisitions are made, the effect of combined modifiers versus individual modifiers should be carefully reviewed.

In the event of mergers, it may be possible to pool the experience of the merging parties. If the pooling of experience will retain favorable modifiers, an attempt should be made to structure the business deal to retain such modifiers.

There can be substantial experience rating effects from the buying and selling of entities. For instance, let's assume that the XYZ Corporation has been a well-managed company and has experienced much lower than average workers compensation losses. The owners of XYZ decided to sell their company to ABC Industries, which unfortunately has a much higher modifier than XYZ. If the purchase price involves some cash or equivalent notes, and the entire transaction takes place on the same day, the ongoing business of XYZ will be subjected to the modifier of ABC Industries, since there was a majority change in ownership on a given day. However, had ABC structured the purchase so that $\frac{1}{3}$ would be purchased one day, $\frac{1}{3}$ the next day, and $\frac{1}{3}$ the ensuing day, on no one given day would there be more than a 50 percent change in ownership. As a result, the experience of XYZ could be pooled with the experience of ABC. Even though the modifier then applied to XYZ would be higher than the previous modifier under the previous ownership, ABC Industries as a group would realize the savings and avoid an immediate discount on the earning stream of XYZ.

Another common example of a change in ownership is the death of a majority owner of the company. Although the rule differs somewhat in different states, the general rule is that upon the death of a principal owner, especially if more than 60 or 70 percent was owned prior to death, a major change of ownership takes place and the modifiers are no longer applicable. With a debit modifier, this could result in substantial savings. On the other hand, if a good modifier is lost, this compounds the already heavy loss of a key person.

It is impossible in this brief section to go into all the fine details of ownership as it relates to experience rating. However, it can be seen that there is a huge opportunity for savings, as well as catastrophic additional premiums, if business organizations don't carefully define the effect of ownership changes on the experience modifiers. Parties considering the purchase or sale of a company, mergers, or spin-offs should employ a knowledgeable person to perform a series of test ratings using various assumptions and make specific recommendations.

55. Correct Calculation Errors

A number of errors can be made when calculating experience modifiers. Some of the most common are reviewed below.

Subrogation Recoveries.   Many injuries to workers are caused by the negligence of third parties. The standard process is for the workers compensation insurance company to pay workers compensation benefits while joining with the injured employee in a liability suit against the party who caused the injury. All the while, the outstanding claim is charged to the insured under the experience rating plan. However, the experience rating rules allow for immediate revision at the time a successful recovery is made on the suit against the third party.

For instance, let's assume that a $90,000 claim has been included in the experience rating plan. The ensuing third-party suit is quite serious and takes 4 years to resolve. In the meantime, the claim has been included in two experience rating modifiers. At the time the claim is resolved, the insured can ask the insurance company to revise all of the current and past experience rating data to reflect the recovery made. In this case, if the entire $90,000 is recovered, with the exception of $15,000 in attorney's fees, the ratable amount will be reduced from $90,000 to $15,000 to reflect the net expense to the insurance company including legal fees.

From time to time, it is advisable for the business manager to review all past claims for the past 5 years to see if any have been successfully subrogated. Then, experience rating data should be checked to see that the experience rating data has been properly revised.

Noncompensable Claims.   Some claims presented to employers by employees may not be compensable. For instance, an employee may sustain an injury at home and try to claim that it was occupationally related. Other examples may be injuries sustained by employees while traveling to and from work. Still others may include aggravated disease and old injury claims. The insurance company, while defending the claim, will also establish a reserve, often on a worst-case basis. This reserve will be maintained until the claim is resolved, often in a court. In the event that the claim is successfully defended, the insured may request the insurance company to refile any and all data which included the disputed claim. Again, a periodic check should be made of all past claims to see if any were in dispute, and if they were successfully defended. If so, past experience rating data should be revised accordingly.

Duplication of Claims and Transposition of Numbers. Out of the billions of characters inputted into the experience rating system, some errors are bound to occur. For instance, a claim of $1,900 could be inputted as $9,100. A $5,000 claim could have an extra zero accidentally added, so that it becomes $50,000. Claims included in experience rating data should be carefully checked for such errors.

Other similar errors involve duplication of claims. For example, a claim might be shown open for $20,000 as of the last valuation date and subsequently be closed for $21,000. The closed amount of $21,000 could be included in the data provided by the insurer without the open reserve of $20,000 being deleted. This would erroneously inflate losses by $20,000.

There have been cases of employees who tried to file the same claims in more than one state. If insurance companies set up two separate files, they may end up showing reserves in two states where only one should be indicated.

When reviewing experience rating calculations, it is important to look for these types of errors by comparing the losses included in the calculation with those included in loss reports provided by the insurer.

Improper Limitation of Losses. Unfortunately, severe losses do occur. If an employee injury results in a quadriplegia, the ultimate loss cost and resulting reserves could range anywhere from $750,000 to $5 million. Obviously, if large, catastrophic losses were charged in their entirety to an insured, the experience modifier that would be developed could cause such exorbitant increases in premiums as to bankrupt the insured. Therefore, experience rating plans allow individual losses to be limited to a certain amount per injured employee, while all multiple employee losses to more than one employee arising out of the same occurrence will be limited to a somewhat higher amount. At the time of this writing, for instance, the per employee limitation in Texas is $83,500 while the overall occurrence limitation is $167,000. In Illinois, the per employee limitation is $121,000 and the overall occurrence limitation is $242,000.

It is this loss limitation feature that causes loss frequency to affect modifiers more than loss severity. All small losses are included in their entirety, while only portions of large losses are included in the formula.

While there have been cases of individual losses that were not properly limited, errors occur more often when a number of employees are injured in the same accident. If proper input is not given to the rating bureau, these losses and loss reserves arising from one occurrence may not be grouped for the overall occurrence limitation. Therefore, if the business manager knows of instances in which several employees were injured in a single accident, the experience rating calculation should be examined to be certain they were all grouped together for the loss limitation instead of being included in their entirety.

Summary. The errors described above should not be viewed as an indictment against the insurance industry. Mistakes can and do happen. While insurance companies and their bureaus should be expected to develop proper experience modifiers, it is also the responsibility of management to carefully monitor this area.

The average employer cannot hope to totally understand the complicated experience rating process. Therefore, it is usually advisable to use and retain insurance agents, brokers, and consultants who are thoroughly familiar with this process.

One of the services a professional agent/broker can and should provide is coordination and review of the experience rating process.

7

Property Insurance

Ever since the first lean-to was built for shelter, people have worried about the elements destroying their property. When the insurance industry began to develop in the late 1700s, the primary subject of insurance was property, such as cargo, homes, buildings, and factories. At first, such coverage was simple. It covered the specific peril of fire. Over time, the market grew and coverages became broader. Windstorm, hail, collapse, theft, vandalism, and other fortuitous causes of loss became covered perils.

Property insurance is first-party coverage, as compared to liability insurance, which is described as third-party coverage. The insurance company, the second party, covers the policyholder, the first party, against damage. Under liability insurance, the insurance company is covering the insured against actions brought by an outside party, usually referred to as a third party. For a third-party policy to pay, there must be negligence involved on the part of the insured. Under first-party coverage, negligence is not an issue. If the property is damaged, and the damage was caused by an insured peril, the first-party policy pays. For most insureds, property insurance premiums are lower than liability and workers compensation premiums. On the other hand, improper coverage can result in catastrophic financial consequences. Therefore, it is usually wise to buy as broad a coverage as possible and, if in doubt, be prepared to overinsure, since any possible premium savings from reduced coverage may not warrant the adverse financial consequences.

Today, there are two basic coverage forms: *named perils* and *all risk*. Named perils coverage is just what its name indicates: it covers, specifically, such named perils as fire, lightning, hail, windstorm, smoke, and explosion. For a claim to be paid, the insured must prove that the damage was caused by the covered peril.

The broader and more desirable form is all risk coverage. In effect, this policy form covers all perils not specifically excluded by the policy. Under this form, the burden of proof shifts to the insurance company. To deny a claim, the insurance company must prove that the peril which caused the loss is specifically excluded by the policy. Otherwise, the company must pay.

Ways to Control Costs

This chapter provides 11 ways to control property insurance costs.

56. Obtain Rate
Deviations/Dividends

Over the passage of time, insurance companies have thoroughly codified the approach to developing rates for different types of structures. For instance, there are higher rates for frame structures and lower rates for concrete structures. These rates are modified according to the type of business carried on by the occupants: for example, a brick company presents a lower risk of fire than a fireworks factory.

In most states, rating bureaus have developed specific rates or "base rates" for each individual commercial building. In developing policy premiums, insurance underwriters begin with these base rates and apply credits and debits to develop a final *manual premium*. Most states allow the insurer to discount these rates up front through the use of "deviations," which can range from 10 percent during tight insurance markets to as much as 75 percent during soft markets.

In addition to, or in some cases in lieu of deviations, some insurance companies will also pay dividends on property insurance premiums after the end of the policy term. To effect the lowest possible premiums, the buyer must review availability and applicability of deviations and dividends.

57. Use Deductibles

As with other coverage lines, deductibles can substantially reduce property insurance premiums. Potential losses must be weighed against premium savings. Specific deductibles may be assumed per item or type of property, per location, or per occurrence.

Some buyers have assumed lower deductibles due to concern over an unexpectedly large number of occurrences in a given policy period. An alternative approach is to purchase aggregate deductible coverage for the year. For instance, a policyholder may assume a $10,000 deductible subject to a maximum annual amount of $30,000. Under this plan, once the deductibles exceed $30,000, all additional amounts are paid by the insurance company. This allows a business to budget for the worst case.

Deductibles may be very desirable if the premium credits allowed justify the additional risk assumed.

58. Invest in Fire Prevention

Steps taken to prevent fires will result in lower insurance premiums. A few suggestions are made below.

Fire Extinguishers.　Virtually every large fire begins as a small fire that grows. Hand extinguishers have prevented many small fires from becoming major ones. As a result, one of the credits allowed is for hand extinguisher units if a proper number of such units are maintained by the policyholder.

The first step in determining the cost-effectiveness of adding extinguishers is to ask your insurance agent or advisor to obtain a copy of the manual rate work sheet. If no extinguisher credits are allowed, recalculate the rates with the appropriate credit and apply them to the insurable values. The difference in premium is the amount of first-year savings that can be compared to the additional cost of acquiring and maintaining the necessary extinguishers. In many instances, no additional units will be required. Upon installation of the units that are required, the governing bureau will promulgate a revised rate.

Sprinklers.　Substantial premium savings are available to owners of medium- and large-sized properties if approved sprinklers are installed. To determine the cost-benefit ratio, two major steps must be taken. First, a major underwriter of "highly protected" risks—such as a Factor Mutual affiliate—should be requested to perform an engineering study to determine the type and size of the sprinkler system that will be required and the resulting estimated premium savings.

With these specifications in hand, two or three sprinkler installation firms should be approached for proposals. If the savings do not totally justify the cost, the owner should negotiate with the insurance company to determine whether it will reduce its requirements subject to minimums required by local governmental units.

Even if the direct savings do not toally justify the cost, consideration should be given to the fact that very few sprinklered properties are ever destroyed by fire. It may be prudent to spend a reasonable sum today to avoid the heart-rending experience of being involved in a major property loss. Also, while it is very costly to equip existing buildings with sprinklers, the cost is much lower in new structures; sprinklers should be considered for them even if not required by building codes.

Hood Systems—Restaurants and Painting Booths.   While it may not be
desirable to equip the entire premises with sprinklers, substantial credits
are available for specialized sprinkler or fire control systems in especially
hazardous areas. For instance, grease will build up in exhaust fans
contained in hoods over restaurant cooking equipment. The fire exposure from the grease can be virtually eliminated through the installation
of special hood systems.

Another example is painting booths. The paint spray may be highly
flammable. Again, special hood systems substantially reduce the possibility of a fire's starting and spreading.

Other special systems are available for other special exposures such as
those presented by data-processing facilities.

Alarm Systems.   Alarm systems, through early warning, can substantially reduce losses resulting from the peril of fire as well as from
burglary and robbery. Based on the exposure and location of the
premises, a loud bell outside the building may be the only requirement.
In other cases, to obtain the maximum credit, a direct line to a central
station with 24-hour monitoring may be required.

Again, the cost of such systems must be weighed against the premium
savings, the availability of insurance, and the inconvenience of a loss.

Insulated Columns of Steel Buildings.   Generally, steel buildings do
not burn. However, if the property inside continues burning over even
a short period of time, the metal supporting beams become so hot that
they buckle and cause the building to collapse.

This collapse exposure can be substantially reduced by shielding the
columns with fireproof insulation during construction (or often some
time after the building has been completed). This usually inexpensive
action will substantially reduce the fire rate.

Fire Doors.   Usually the highest rated activity or highest rated construction materials are used to determine the insurance rates for contiguous
structures unless the exposure is segregated. The most common method
of segregating the exposure is to install fire doors which will contain the
fire in a specific area. In other words, the fire is prevented from
traveling to other parts of the premises. This allows different rates to be
applied to different parts of the premises.

Fire Hydrants.   Often, new buildings are located on the edge of the
community and may not be near a fire hydrant. As a result, adequate

water may not be available to fight a fire if one occurs. Consequentially, fire rates are surcharged.

As the community grows and new fire hydrants are installed, adequate water supplies become available. However, the fire rate surcharge may not be dropped unless the bureau is notified.

If a rate surcharge exists for a building, an effort should be made to encourage the city to install a fire hydrant nearby. Once the hydrant is in place, the bureau should be advised immediately.

Review of Fire Rating Schedule. There are numerous other credits that are available and debits that may be applied in determining property insurance rates. For instance, using metal shelving rather than wood can make a substantial difference. The departure of certain neighboring firms can also affect rates. For example, if a former neighbor was in the furniture-refinishing business, a high exposure rate would have affected your rating. If the new neighbor is in ceramic tile sales, you should file for a lower rate.

Business managers should review the rate schedules with their insurance agents or advisors to determine what credits might be available and what surcharges might be avoided. Remember, not only will the building rate be reduced, but so will rates for all other property coverages—such as the rates on contents and business interruption.

59. Use Business Interruption Reporting Form

Business interruption coverage is a form of disability coverage for a commercial entity when its property is damaged. If an adequate limit of coverage is not in force at the time of a loss, substantial penalties may be imposed by the insurance company. Since business operations fluctuate during the year, higher than necessary limits for slow periods may be carried if the coverage limits are established once a year based on peak periods. However, coverage only reimburses the insured for actual losses, so no "gain" would be experienced should a loss occur during a slow period.

To enable the insured to have appropriate coverage at all times without wasting premium dollars, the insurance industry has developed a *reporting form* policy. Under this approach, the insured sets a maximum limit such as, for example, 125 percent of the highest peak period. Actual business volume is reported each month, and the premium is adjusted to reflect the actual business activity for the previous 12 months.

60. Store Volatiles Safely

Many buildings will have a substantial surcharge to the base rate if volatile or highly flammable materials are stored on premises. If such materials are stored, consideration should be given to several methods of preventing the losses and reducing insurance premiums.

First, is storage of the materials absolutely necessary to efficient operation of the business? If not, determine whether a supplier can store such materials until they are needed.

If storage of the materials on premises is desirable or necessary, can they be stored in an outbuilding? In that case, the surcharge would be applied *only* to that small structure and could be deleted from the much larger building.

If continuous use of the material is necessary, can it be stored in an underground tank outside the building and simply pumped in as needed, with automatic shut-off valves? This method should also result in a reduced premium on the main building.

Again, the cost of these approaches must be weighed against the positive factors.

61. Buy Underwriters Laboratory-Approved UL-90 Roof

In areas prone to severe windstorms, roof damage is a major concern of insurance companies. If a roof is installed or modified to meet the standards of a UL-90 roof, substantial credits are usually available. Basically, such a roof involves extra bolts to keep it from taking off like a kite.

62. Use Fireproof Cabinets

Valuable papers, records, and accounts receivable are the heart of today's business. Industry statistics indicate that almost one-half of the businesses that lose their accounts receivable through fire or other perils never reopen.

While it is extremely important to carry proper coverage for this property, it is even more desirable to avoid damage in the first place. Therefore, valuable papers, computer tapes, and accounts receivable records should be stored in fireproof cabinets, safes, or vaults. Substantial premium credits are then applied to the valuable papers and accounts receivable insurance.

63. Get Duplicate Records Credit

For various reasons, duplicate records may be kept off premises. For instance, accounting work is done off premises or the firm's accounts receivable are used as collateral for a bank loan. In the event of a loss, the records could easily be reproduced using such duplicate records.

Probably the best loss control device for use with accounts receivable and other valuable records is to make duplicate records and store them off site. The records should be updated frequently. This approach should also be used with computer data.

Generally, there is a credit of up to 50 percent for duplicate records.

64. Obtain Coinsurance Credits

Of all property losses, probably 90 percent are under $20,000. One could reason that a $20,000 policy would cover the vast majority of losses. However, if all business only carried these low limits, the rates per $100 of covered limits would be substantially higher. In addition, there would be no coverage for the large catastrophic losses that do occur.

In order to collect enough premiums to cover small and large losses, insurance companies offer lower rates to firms that carry insurance "to value"—in other words, limits which are 80, 90, or 100 percent of the actual exposure. The higher the percentage, usually referred to as the "coinsurance percentage," the lower the rate.

However, if the insured has fudged or simply fails to carry the proper limits, a coinsurance penalty will be imposed in the event of a loss.

To illustrate how a coinsurance penalty operates, let's assume that a building is worth $1 million and that the insured accepts a rate based on a 100 percent coinsurance clause and that, however, the insured decides to carry only $800,000 of insurance. During the term, a $100,000 loss occurs. The claim payment will be based on the following:

$$\frac{\$800,000 \text{ (insurance carried)}}{\$1,000,000 \text{ (insurance required)}} = 80\% \times \$100,000$$
$$= 80,000 \text{ (insurance recovery)}$$

In this example, the coinsurance penalty is $20,000.

The recommended approach is to accept lower rates based on a coinsurance clause and then be careful to insure to the stipulated percentage. It may be wise to select limits that are 5 percent more than the coinsurance clause. For instance, if 80 percent coinsurance is selected, then select a limit based on 85 percent of the insurable value.

In many cases, insurance companies will agree to waive any coinsurance penalties if the initial values are documented as being similar to those required. This is called an *agreed amount* clause.

65. Use Reporting Policies

Another way for businesses with fluctuating values to avoid a coinsurance penalty is to negotiate a reporting form for buildings and contents. This allows the business to have the maximum credits based on a 100 percent coinsurance clause while purchasing an exact amount of coverage.

66. Report Proper Builders Risk Values

A builders risk policy covers new buildings and additions to existing buildings during the construction phase. Such a policy is also subject to coinsurance clauses, usually with a 100 percent value requirement.

The total cost associated with the building may not be the proper limit to select. Architectural fees are usually excluded from values used to select a limit. If the building is damaged by windstorm, for example, no additional design work will be required to reconstruct it. In addition, some items such as site preparation, parking lots, driveways, curbing, sidewalks, fencing, and light posts may not be covered by the policy and therefore values should be excluded.

In summary, only the value of covered work should be reported in developing the values on which builders risk premiums will be based.

8

Insurance Industry Relationships

In the United States, property and liability insurance is distributed by three types of systems: the direct writer system, the exclusive agency system, and the independent agency system. The direct writers and exclusive agency insurance companies market insurance through salaried salespeople or commissioned agents who sell only the insurance products of a particular company. Examples of direct writers and exclusive agency companies include Employers of Wausau, Liberty Mutual, Nationwide, State Farm, American Mutual, Farmers Group, and Sentry Insurance. The agency system insurance companies, on the other hand, depend upon independent insurance agents and brokers to sell their products. These agents or brokers often represent many insurance companies. A few examples of the many agency system insurance companies include: Aetna, American International Group, Chubb, CIGNA, Continental, Crum & Forster, Hartford, Kemper, Reliance, Safeco, Travelers, and United States Fidelity & Guaranty (USF&G).

From the standpoint of the insurance buyer, each of these alternatives for marketing insurance has advantages and disadvantages as compared to the other. Probably the principal advantages of the direct writer–exclusive agency system over the independent agency system are the higher quality claims, loss prevention, rehabilitation, and similar services typically provided by these companies. On the other hand, the sales representatives of direct writers and exclusive agency companies are typically not as skilled and knowledgeable as independent agents and brokers. In addition, direct writers and exclusive agency companies representatives can offer only the services and products that their employer provides.

Probably the most important advantage of using independent agents and brokers—as compared to direct writers and exclusive agents—is the fact that agents and brokers can place insurance with any one company or a combination of many insurance companies with which they do business. Not being employees of the insurance company, some independent agents and brokers are more oriented toward representing the buyer of insurance than the insurance company. The insurance buyer should, however, keep in mind that an insurance agent is legally an agent of the insurance company and not of the insurance buyer.

An insurance buyer can have success using either the American agency system or the direct writer/exclusive agency system. The main point to remember is that the agent/broker or insurance company representative is your primary interface/supplier of your insurance protection, and it is therefore important to choose a representative that can best serve your interests.

Agent/Broker Compensation

The compensation paid to independent agents or brokers by the businesses that they insure can be in the form of commissions paid by the insurance company and passed through as part of the premium, a fee paid directly by the insured business, or a combination of the two. Commissions vary from insurance company to insurance company, agent to agent, and region to region. In general, however, insurance companies will pay a commission of around 16 percent of the premium on commercial auto insurance, 19 percent on commercial fire insurance, 19 percent on commercial general liability, 18 percent on commercial package policies, and 10 percent on workers compensation. Risk managers of larger businesses may have the bargaining power to negotiate the commission percentage with their agent or broker, and sometimes an agent or broker will accept reduced commissions from the insurance company in order to compete on medium-sized accounts against other agents and brokers in a competitive bidding situation. If the agent or broker is receiving commission income from the insurance company rather than a fee from the insured, the insured should request an annual statement from the agent or broker regarding the income received from the insurer. This information should be helpful in evaluating the services of the agent or broker.

Business managers of medium-sized and large businesses may be able to negotiate with their agent or broker to operate on a fee basis. This could be a negotiated flat fee or a fee based on time and expense. Since income to the agent or broker computed in this manner is not a function of the insurance premium, possible disincentives to reducing premiums that are inherent to the commission system are eliminated. This approach can also smooth out the agent's/broker's income rather than having it subject to the cyclical nature of the insurance business. One problem, however, in attempting to place agents/brokers on such a system is that they are not accustomed to accounting for their time and expenses and frequently do not have the systems in place to do so properly.

Arranging Coverage and Determining Premiums

The process generally used to purchase insurance is illustrated in Figure 8.1. The insured asks an agent or broker to obtain a quotation. Underwriting data necessary to determine whether or not the risk is insurable is assembled by the insured and the agent. The agent may or may not then ask a *surplus lines broker* to assist in approaching insurers. Surplus lines brokers are most often used for specialty coverages (e.g., professional liability, aircraft insurance, and marine insurance) or for insureds who are in very high-risk businesses (e.g., chemical, pharmaceutical, or pollution cleanup). The independent agent and surplus lines broker are usually paid commissions from the insurance premium.

An *underwriter* at the insurance company reviews the underwriting data and determines whether the company wants to write the policy.

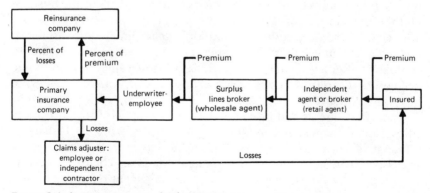

Figure 8.1. Insurance process—distribution system

The underwriter who decides to write the policy also decides how the premium will be determined. Rating technicians generally do the actual mechanics based on the underwriter's instructions. Sometimes, particularly with large accounts, the local branch office underwriter must seek home office approval of a decision. Note that the underwriter does not become involved in paying claims. For this reason, all understandings related to the insurance coverage should be put in writing.

Often, the insurer wants to write a particular policy but does not want to bear the responsibility of paying all the losses. In such a situation, the insurer may arrange with one or more *reinsurers* to share a portion of the premium and of the insured losses. Usually, the insured will not know whether or not its risks are reinsured and, if so, who the reinsurers are. The primary insurer is the only party to the insurance contract with the insured and bears all responsibility for insured losses, whether or not the reinsurer(s) pays. The claims process, also illustrated in Figure 8.1, is reviewed in Chapter 9.

Ways to Reduce Costs

This chapter gives seven ways to reduce costs by understanding the working relationships in the insurance industry.

67. Choose a Knowledgeable Agent or Broker

One of the most effective steps a business manager can take to reduce business insurance costs is to choose an insurance agent or broker who can best serve the organization's needs. The individual(s) and the individual's firm represent the business entity to the insurance community, handle hundreds, thousands, or millions of dollars of the business entity's funds in the form of insurance premiums, provide consultative advice on how to protect the organization's continuing financial stability, and negotiate on behalf of the business entity to recover from insurance companies after a loss has occurred. This individual and this firm should be chosen as carefully as one would choose an accountant, attorney, or investment advisor.

Too often, agents and brokers are chosen because of social relationships rather than ability to do the job. This is particularly true in family-held businesses. In large businesses that have full-time professional risk managers, senior management should also be careful not to undermine the effectiveness of its risk management department as a result of social relationships with the agent/broker. Some agents/brokers will attempt to "go over the risk manager's head," and this can cost the organization considerable amounts of money if not properly handled by senior management. A similar problem occurs when the agent/broker is chosen because of a business relationship. For example, banks often succumb to an agent's offer to deposit large funds in exchange for some or all of the "insurance pie." Only in very rare situations will an agent or broker chosen or retained solely because of family, social, or business relationships perform the quality services deserved by a particular organization. Frequently, the agent/broker becomes complacent and fails to provide proper service.

A business that has grown rapidly over the years can actually outgrow the capability of its agent or broker. In this situation, the agent or broker was possibly well qualified in the early days of the business. The business grew over time, however, and the insurance industry changed dramatically. Agents and brokers must continually educate themselves and keep up to date on developments in the insurance industry as well as the industries in which their clients are engaged in business. A new agent or broker should be found if the organization outgrows the capability of its agent/broker or if the agent/broker fails to stay on top of industry developments.

Many factors may be used to assist in the selection of an agent/broker. Some of the more important ones include: industry expertise, experience, general insurance knowledge, access to insurance markets, and staff support.

Industry expertise of an agent/broker involves knowledge of your business and the industry in which it operates. This type of knowledge pays off in proper insurance coverages. It also ensures, from a pricing perspective, knowledge of insurance and relationships with the insurance companies most interested in writing insurance for businesses in the industry. When interviewing an agent/broker, you can generally assume industry expertise if the agent/broker has a large book of business within the same industry.

Overall experience in insurance and risk management within the geographical area of operations may also be very important. Agents/brokers who have been doing business within the geographical area for a long period of time and also have clients in the same industry fall into this category. It is most important, when trying to choose a new agent/broker, to obtain and talk with references.

While there may be certain advantages in being the largest account written by an agency or brokerage firm, there is usually more to be gained from being one of a number of large accounts. It is important to interview references from accounts of similar size and complexity handled by the agent/broker.

General insurance knowledge of the agent/broker obviously is extremely important to the business. Although a substantial amount of experience is quite important, it should not be the only factor used to determine general insurance knowledge since the industry changes rapidly and some people simply have not kept up with the changes. To evaluate superior general insurance knowledge, find out whether the agent/broker attends industry seminars, participates in industry seminars as a speaker or lecturer, and/or has published articles for trade magazines. Participation on insurance committees of trade associations inside or outside the insurance industry is also a very good indicator of knowledge and capability. In addition, professional designations such as, in order of priority, Chartered Property–Casualty Underwriter (CPCU), Certified Insurance Counselor (CIC), Accredited Advisor in Insurance (AAI), and Associate in Risk Management (ARM) attest to a general competency in the field of property casualty insurance. While not quite as difficult, these programs resemble the Certified Public Accountant (CPA) designation in that they involve the passing of nationally administered examinations.

Access to insurance markets, and clout with them, is one of the most important factors to consider when relying on an agent/broker in lieu of using direct writers, affecting both the price and the coverage terms that can be negotiated. When talking with an agent/broker about the possibility of writing a firm's insurance, you should discuss the insurance marketplace. Determine how many insurance companies the agency typically does business with, the most predominant insurance companies used by the agency, and—if the firm's insurance involves any unusual insurance policies, such as professional liability insurance—the amount of experience the agent/broker has in the specialty coverage marketplace ("excess and surplus lines [E&S]insurance").

Staff support available to the agent/broker, the size of the agency/brokerage firm itself, affects service. Determine what support the individual primarily responsible for your account has in the areas of marketing (selling your risks to insurance companies), administration (e.g., accounting and billing), and account servicing (e.g., issuing of certificates, reviewing audits and experience rating data, and checking insurance policies). Access to an assistant or a support staff to help with these functions will greatly increase the agent/broker's time available for more creative work on the account.

68. Use a Limited Number of Agencies/Brokerages

For routine commercial accounts, a single agent/broker or a single direct writer should be used to provide all of the property and casualty insurance. The use of a single representative substantially increases the insured's clout with that firm, avoids coordination problems that may arise when several firms are used, and makes the account more important to the agent/broker because of the volume of revenues that it provides.

Larger corporations sometimes use more than one firm to represent them in the insurance marketplace. Many corporate insurance buyers of large organizations will use two agents/brokers to maintain a certain level of constant competition on the account. When an organization has numerous complicated insurance needs, it also makes sense to use several brokers that have expertise in some of the complicated areas. For example, an organization with both national and international exposures might determine that it is in its best interest to use one agent/broker for the domestic insurance program and a separate one for the international program. Another logical split might be to use one agent/broker for all property coverages and another for all liability coverages.

The organization should never allow an agent's association or insurance placement committee to place its insurance. This process, which has most often been used by nonprofit and governmental entities, allows a number of agencies to place insurance and split the commission income. This will almost always result in a total lack of competition, higher premiums, reduced service levels, and uncoordinated coverages.

In summary, very few, if any, organizations can justify using more than four different firms to place their property and casualty insurance. Most organizations should use only one. When more than one agent or broker is used, the organization will experience the following costs and potential problems:

- Additional administrative time and effort in coordinating the activities of the agents
- Possible gaps in coverage from uncoordinated policies
- Possible loss of bargaining power with insurers because of reduced premium volume under control of each agent
- Possible lower service levels from agents because of reduced commissions as compared to what would be received if the entire account were controlled

69. Use a Written Scope of Engagement

The agent/broker is paid a fairly substantial amount of money in the form of commissions or fees to service a business entity's insurance account. This often involves much behind-the-scenes work of which the business manager is not even aware. One of the most frequent causes of dissatisfaction on the part of the business manager is the feeling that the agent/broker is not providing the services that the firm needs. To ensure that the organization is getting its money's worth from its agent/broker, it is strongly advised that a written account service agreement be negotiated with and executed by the agent/broker. Having a written agreement gives the business manager a standard by which to measure the agent's/broker's service levels and provides the agent/broker with a means to justify income levels generated on the account.

The written scope of engagement and the agent's/broker's commissions or fees should be discussed, renegotiated, and revised on an annual basis. This approach will help the organization to get its money's worth.

70. Maintain Communication

Tied into service levels of the agent/broker is formal communication between the business manager and the insurance representative. To provide high quality services, the agent/broker needs a substantial amount of information from the client. From the business manager's perspective, needs change during the year, other business functions (such as budgeting) can be affected by changes in the insurance industry, and business environment changes necessitate adjustments in the insurance program.

To facilitate interaction between the agent/broker and the business manager, it is strongly suggested that an annual meeting be held prior to the business's insurance renewals. The timing of the meeting will vary somewhat with the size and complexity of the firm's insurance program, but it should generally take place between 90 and 120 days prior to renewal.

During the meeting, the business manager should be prepared to provide the agent/broker with updated underwriting information (e.g., forecasted annual sales, payrolls, and number of vehicles for the next 12 months, information on any new properties which might be acquired, and planned changes in business activities). The agent/broker should be prepared to inform the business manager of the current status of the insurance marketplace, the planned approach to the insurance marketplace for the renewal of the account, and an expectation of premium levels for the next 12 months.

For all but the smallest commercial accounts, quarterly meetings should also be held with the agent/broker. The agenda for these meetings will vary with the activities and needs of the business and the agent/broker. However, topics to be covered should include a review of open claims, updated information on business activities of the insured, a review of renewal insurance policies when received from the insurance companies, a brief review of experience rating, annual audit, and—if applicable—retrospective rating calculations when received; the general status of the insurance marketplace should also be discussed to avoid surprises if there are any changes.

All too often, business managers meet with their agent/broker only when coerced into doing so by the agent/broker. To these people, insurance is a necessary evil and time spent discussing it is time wasted. Regularly scheduled meetings are extremely important, however, to ensure that the agent/broker is staying on track, that actions taken to deal with insurance marketplace changes are proactive rather than reactive, and that factors which may affect the firm's insurance costs are dealt with before it is too late.

71. Know Your Underwriter

Business managers of medium-sized and large commercial firms should meet and get to know the underwriter(s) for the major lines of insurance purchased by the business. In risk management and insurance, relationships can be very important when negotiating cost and coverage. The business manager knows the firm's operations and industry much better than the agent/broker and is in a position to communicate information that will positively affect the underwriter's decision making.

Some agents/brokers will resist the client's attempts to get to know the underwriter. Usually, this is caused by an agent's/broker's unfounded insecurity and desire to avoid the development of relationships that will lessen the business manager's dependency. However, some underwriters truly have no desire to meet with their insureds, and forcing the issue in this situation can be counterproductive.

When a meeting is arranged, the agent/broker and business manager should discuss the meeting in advance and develop a strategy for it. Keep in mind that the agent/broker already knows the underwriter and can give valuable advice on how to best achieve your objectives.

72. Negotiate Fees/Commissions

The agent's/broker's compensation package should be tied in with the written scope of engagement: when the scope of engagement is drafted and executed, the agent's/broker's compensation should also be discussed and negotiated. The scope of engagement provides a blueprint upon which the appropriate compensation package can be composed.

Compensation plans vary; but they generally involve fees, commissions, or a combination of the two. A survey to which 205 risk managers responded illustrates the various types of compensation arrangements actually used by practicing risk managers. These arrangements include commissions which are sometimes negotiated, flat fees, and time and expense billings. Responses to this question on the survey are summarized in Table 8.1.

Even if a straight commission arrangement is used, the business manager should demand to be told the amount of commission received by the agent. The commission may then be negotiated or, at the very least, the agent can be required to perform services commensurate with the level of income provided.

73. Use Consultants

In the early to mid-1970s, a new type of professional insurance advisor emerged—the risk management and insurance consultant. Today, there are well over 100 risk management and insurance consulting firms in the United States. Typically, a risk management consulting firm employs a number of individuals with substantial experience in insurance and/or risk management, and it provides various services to insurance buyers for a fee. Organizations that cannot afford to hire a full-time risk manager can often save substantially more money than the consulting fee and, more important, can rest assured that a responsive insurance and risk management program is in place by retaining a consultant.

The services usually offered by these consultants include such things as insurance policy coverage and cost reviews, review and feedback on corporate risk management programs, and alternative risk financing plan feasibility studies (e.g., captive and self-insurance feasibility studies). Consulting firms can also prepare insurance specifications and assist in bidding the insurance program.

Since the risk management consulting industry is subject to virtually no regulation, business managers should be quite careful when choosing a consultant. First determine whether the consultant sells insurance.

Table 8.1 Use of Fees versus Commissions by Risk Managers

Arrangement	Use	Do not use
Commissions—not negotiated	57%	41%
Commissions—negotiated	33%	66%
Negotiated fees	34%	63%
Fees based on time and expense	13%	84%
Insurance placed net of commission	22%	75%

SOURCE: Frederic C. Church, Jr., "The 'Compleat' Risk Manager," *Risk Management*, July 1984, p. 35.

Hiring an organization that does sell insurance can create severe conflicts of interest and mitigate the positive effects of the consulting engagement. If a potential consultant does also sell insurance, the manager is strongly advised to execute an agreement that the consultant will not act as an agent or broker on behalf of the business entity. Furthermore, the business manager should resist all temptation to use that individual as an agent or broker for at least a 3- to 5-year period following the consulting engagement.

Other factors that affect the selection of a consultant are substantially similar to those that should be relied upon in selecting an agent or broker. Verify that the consultant has substantial experience and knowledge of insurance and risk management, especially in working for clients in your industry or a similar industry, and a good reputation for a quality work product. Obtain a number of references and telephone them to query the results of the consultant's work on their accounts.

Generally speaking, the consultant's fee is based on the time involved in performing a consulting project. The larger firms use a number of individuals with specialized expertise relevant to the project. When hiring a consultant, be wary of organizations that use a highly experienced principal to sell consulting jobs and then rely on much less experienced staff to perform the work. Make sure you know exactly who will be doing the consulting work and evaluate his or her ability to perform it.

Once a year, *Business Insurance* magazine publishes a list of United States risk management consultants which summarizes their services and capabilities. Since many public libraries subscribe to this magazine, the business manager can use the list to identify possible consultants to retain.

9
Claims

When losses occur, insurance companies are expected to respond in a professional manner to rapidly settle the resulting claim or claims. Claims are the major cost element in insurance premiums and the reason businesses purchase insurance. Depending upon the line of insurance, claims costs generally represent between 50 and 90 percent of the premium dollar.

For all but the very smallest commercial insureds, insurance is simply a cost-stabilizing device. Most insureds will eventually pay all of their losses back to insurance companies in the form of premium dollars. This becomes most obvious in the liability lines (e.g., workers compensation, auto, and general liability) wherein experience rating, retrospective rating, and other loss-sensitive rating programs make the impact of claims on ultimate premiums quite visible. However, this general rule is also true in other lines of insurance, such as property insurance.

Workers compensation and liability insurance claims cost includes not only the amount actually paid in claims but also an estimation of what will be paid on open claims (i.e., those claims that have not been closed through settlement or litigation). This estimate, which is made by the claims adjuster, is called a *case reserve*. The total amount of case reserves is included in *incurred losses*. Incurred losses are given to competing insurers quoting on the insured's account, used to calculate workers compensation experience rating modifiers, and used in calculating premiums under a retrospective rating plan. Therefore, these estimated case reserves have a substantial effect on premiums, and any "overre-serving" done by the insurer will cause undeserved, often unrecoverable, premium increases. Premium costs can be controlled by monitoring and negotiating reserves.

Claims-Adjusting Process

When the insured suffers a loss, a claim is made to the insurance company. Except for very small claims, in which agents are sometimes given settlement authority by insurers, a claims adjuster is assigned to the case by the insurer. The adjuster may be an employee of the insurer, or the insurer may contract with an outside service company to perform this service. Either way, the adjuster's primary allegiance is to the insurer.

As illustrated in Figure 9.1, the adjuster investigates the loss and compares the facts of the case to the terms of the insurance policy. If the adjuster determines that the policy does not cover the loss, the claim is denied. If the adjuster determines that the loss is covered, the adjuster will negotiate with the insured to settle a property claim or with the claimant to settle a liability or workers compensation claim. In the case of potentially severe liability claims, the adjuster will retain a law firm to investigate, defend, and/or settle.

The agent/broker will usually work with the insured to present the claim to the insurer. However, the agent or broker ordinarily cannot commit the insurer to a particular response. Likewise, the underwriter who negotiated the insurance policy does not normally become involved in the claims-adjusting process.

Because claims costs are such a large percentage of the insurance premium, they should be monitored, evaluated, and managed. In the area of property insurance, claims recoveries are also negotiable with the insurance company, and the business manager must work to present the organization's case to the insurance company so as to maximize a recovery following a loss. Since paid claims in the area of workers compensation and liability insurance will directly affect premium costs in the future, the business manager should monitor the loss adjustment

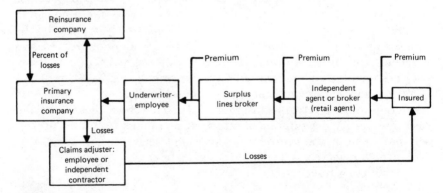

Figure 9.1. Insurance process—claims.

activity of the insurance company to ensure that only legitimate claims are paid, that unpaid claims are not being overreserved, and that claims costs are accurately recorded.

Ways to Reduce Costs

This chapter presents six ways to reduce cost by monitoring claims activities.

74. Request Advance Payment of Property Claims

Insurance covering physical damage to property (e.g., building, contents, and inventory) will indemnify the insured for the costs incurred in repairing or replacing damaged or destroyed property. Usually, insurance companies wait until the property has been repaired or replaced and then reimburse the insured for the costs incurred. However, following a major loss, ask the insurance company to provide an advance payment of the loss. Most reputable insurance companies provide an advance of 75 to 80 percent of the expected loss. These funds are then available for the insured to use in repairing or replacing the property, and the insured, rather than the insurer, will benefit from investment income on the funds during the period of restoration or repair.

75. Use Public Adjusters on Large Property Losses

When a business suffers a large property loss, strong consideration should be given to retaining a reputable public adjuster to represent the business in negotiations with the insurance company. This is particularly true if the loss involves a business interruption claim. The public adjuster will assist the insured in preparing a proof of loss and in negotiating with the insurance company's adjusters. Generally, the public adjuster's compensation will be based upon a per diem fee or a percentage of the final loss recovery. A good public adjuster will almost always recoup far more from the insurer than is spent on the fees.

76. Have Periodic Meetings with Insurance Company Adjusters

Insurance company claims adjusters perform an extremely important task and are an extremely overworked group of people. For example, a workers compensation adjuster may, at any one point in time, have responsibility for 225 open claims.

The insured that takes an interest in its claims services will frequently receive superior service, which will ultimately result in lower claims costs. For this reason, it is suggested that a periodic (e.g., quarterly, semiannual, or annual) meeting be held with the claims administrator in charge of the organization's claims at the insurance company. The status of the firm's largest open claims should be discussed during the meeting. This would include the amount reserved for these claims, actions that have been taken by the adjuster, and settlement strategies. In the area of workers compensation, particularly, careful attention should be paid to reserves for open claims since they will be used in the experience rating (see Chapter 6) and, if applicable, incurred loss retrospective rating (see Chapter 10) calculations.

77. Obtain Right to Approve Workers Compensation and Liability Claims

Workers compensation, automobile, and general liability policies provide the insurance company with the right to dispose of claims as it sees fit. In other words, the insurance contracts do not require the insurance company to consult with the insured in determining whether to attempt to settle a claim or fight it. While in many cases the action taken by the insurance company is in both its and its insured's best interests, there may be exceptions. Probably the most common problem area involves small, what the insurance companies call "nuisance," claims. Often, it costs the insurance company less money to settle a small (e.g., under $1,000), though questionable, claim than it does in attorney fees to fight it, and many insurers will pay these claims. When viewed on an individual claim basis, this approach appears to be logical. However, news travels fast within the plaintiff's bar, and an insurer or self-insured that adopts this philosophy will soon find itself inundated with small nuisance claims. On the other hand, the organization that fights these types of claims will find that the plaintiff's bar quickly loses interest in bringing such suits against it, and the frequency will reduce dramatically over time.

While it is sometimes difficult to negotiate a policy provision requiring insurers to consult with insureds before settling with claimants, many will informally agree to do so. Seek to obtain an agreement with the insurance company wherein your approval will be sought before any claim of less than a prespecified dollar amount (e.g., $1,000 or $2,500) is settled. Then, strongly consider fighting all small claims in which the organization's legal liability is questionable.

78. Audit Claims Departments

Medium-sized and large insureds and self-insureds should strongly consider arranging for periodic audits of workers compensation and liability claim files held by the insurance company or claims administrator.

The claims auditor will review the workload(s) of the claims adjuster(s) primarily responsible for the account, the thoroughness of the investigation of claims, the degree of documentation, and the reserving practices. The claims auditor will also verify the accuracy of reported payments and reserves as well as the adequacy or excessiveness of payments. The claims audit process will involve reviewing 20 percent or more of the open claim files as well as a number of closed claim files. The auditor will analyze loss reserving patterns (e.g., whether closed claims were consistently over- or underreserved), reconcile reported payments or reserves with the claims files, and review other procedures and controls in place.

For organizations that purchase insurance, claims auditors will occasionally find the following types of errors: typographical errors overstating actual claims paid, consistent overreserving which leads to higher-than-deserved experience modifiers or lower-than-deserved retrospective rating returns, payment of frivolous claims, and failure to recognize and/or pursue subrogation possibilities to recover claims dollars.

79. Maintain Loss Records

Many business managers make the mistake of not demanding periodic (e.g., monthly, quarterly, semiannual, or annual) loss reports from their workers compensation, auto, and general liability insurers. This information is invaluable in analyzing safety and loss control programs, in verifying the accuracy of experience rating and retrospective rating calculations, and in obtaining insurance quotations from competing insurance companies. The last use of this data, of course, is one reason why insurers are often reluctant to provide it to insureds. Obviously, it may also be used when negotiating premium costs with the current insurance company.

In addition to providing liability insurance loss data for the current policy year, the insurance company should be requested to provide updated, currently valued loss reports for each of the past 5 years on an annual basis. In other words, a business manager should request 1987 loss data not only in 1987 but also in 1988, 1989, 1990, 1991, and 1992. The total dollars of losses will be different in each of these years as open claims are settled for either more or less than they were originally reserved in 1987. When negotiating with the current insurer or attempting to place coverage with another insurer, it will be important to have the most up-to-date information possible.

In addition, obtaining this information on an annual basis will allow you to review the reserving practices of your insurance company. If the total dollar losses for individual years continually decline as claims mature, there is an indication that the insurance company is consistently overreserving open claims. Since experience rating formulas and some retrospective rating formulas include reserves on open claims in their calculations, this practice will result in overpayment of premiums which might otherwise never be refunded to the insured. If such overreserving practices are discovered, it may be possible to negotiate lower case reserves which will reduce experience modifiers and/or increase retrospective rating returns.

10

Risk Financing

The insurance mechanism is a process in which the premiums of the many pay for the losses of the few. This concept is especially applicable to personal lines insurance and insurance for small companies. However, as companies grow, insurance becomes more of an expense-smoothing mechanism. Over the long run, large insureds will reimburse their insurance companies for all losses, plus expenses, as well as profits. At the same time, the insurance companies may retain the investment income generated as a result of the cash flow. Therefore, as premiums grow for a particular insured, the situation changes to one where the premiums of the one pay the losses of the one.

There are three basic sources of potential profits available to an insurance company: underwriting income, investment income, and capital appreciation. *Underwriting income* is the difference between premiums earned and losses incurred plus expenses. In recent years, insurers have had underwriting losses rather than profits. For example, the industry incurred an estimated $24.9 billion loss in 1985.[1] *Investment income* is earned on funds held by insurers and includes dividends on common stock, interest from bonds, etc. Keep in mind that, while premiums to fund losses are paid at policy inception, losses are not paid until claims are eventually settled or adjudicated. Insurers invest the reserves to pay future claims and derive substantial income from these investments. For example, property-casualty insurers enjoyed investment income of about $19.5 billion in 1985.[2] The third source of income, which has taken on a greater importance during the past few

---

[1]*Operating Results, Year-End 1985 Analysis,* Insurance Services Office, Inc., March 28, 1986, p. 3.

[2]Ibid.

years, is *tax credits and capital gains*. For instance, in 1985 this source added $7.4 billion to the insurance industry's bottom line.[3] Without this source of income, the industry as a whole would have lost money in 1985. In negotiating insurance, particularly for the larger insured, these three sources of income must be understood and taken into account.

Importance of Insurance Cash Flow

As implied above, there are often significant time lags between acts that may lead to legal liability and the settlement or payment of the resulting claims. These time lags are caused by:

- Delays by plaintiffs in reporting and filing claims
- Delays in settlement from the slowness of the legal process
- Delays in cash payments after settlement (particularly for claims that result in periodic payments in the workers compensation area)

The party that holds these funds, whether the insurer or insured, benefits from their income-generating capability. In the early days of insurance and risk management, insurers demanded that annual premiums be paid at policy inception and therefore enjoyed all of the cash flow benefits. In the 1970s and 1980s, however, insurance buyers became more concerned with risk cash flow, with which party the funds were held until paid, and insurers began sharing it.

Now there are various ways that insureds can participate in the investment-income-earning ability of unpaid claims reserves. These plans are available from insurers and may be simple, such as an agreement to pay premiums monthly instead of at policy inception, or they may be quite complex—as will be seen when compensating balance plans are discussed.

There are also risk-financing plans in which insurers do not play a dominant role. The most predominant of these plans are captive insurers, self-insurance, and group pooling.

Rating Plans

The basis of any "cash flow" risk financing plan purchased from an insurance company is the rating plan used. Virtually all cash flow programs are variations on one of two themes: guaranteed cost rating or retrospective rating. Until the mid-1950s, the most common approach to

[3]Ibid.

financing risk was through a *guaranteed cost insurance* program. Under this approach, the insured pays a predetermined premium that stays the same regardless of the losses covered by the policy. In effect, the insurance company takes all risks of loss when this type of insurance is purchased. As premiums began to grow in the United States, particularly in the workers compensation area, a growing demand developed for cost-plus programs which would allow the insured to share some risk with the insurance company. While large insureds were able to negotiate these types of plans from Lloyd's of London and a few U.S. insurance companies, such plans were not available to the average American business. To meet this growing need, the U.S. insurance industry developed a formal cost-plus program which was christened *retrospective rating*.

As with a guaranteed cost rating plan, a premium is developed at the inception of the retrospective rating policy period. However, this premium is only provisional and is subject to a cost-plus calculation which will reflect actual loss experience. Approximately 6 months after the end of the policy period, the insurance company will look back and compare the actual premiums earned to the losses incurred (paid and reserved claims) and recalculate the premium. Subject to an agreed-upon minimum, the insured will receive a return premium if losses are lower than expected. On the other hand, if losses exceed original expectations, additional premiums will be paid by the insured subject to the maximum. Figure 10.1 contains a brief glossary of retrospective rating terms and an illustration of the retrospective rating formula. Unfortunately, many people view retrospective rating plans as being very complicated and, in some cases, punitive. However, this is a fairly simple cost-plus plan and should be viewed as a positive management tool for midsized to larger corporations that wish to control their insurance costs through positive actions.

Generally, retrospective rating plans can be written on 1- or 3-year terms. They often apply to workers compensation, general liability, and automobile exposures. Other lines—such as burglary, plate glass, and other casualty exposures—can also be included. A general rule of thumb is that a business should be paying at least $200,000 in subject premium (i.e., the premium that would be subject to the plan) before the retrospective rating plan becomes a viable option.

Before purchasing a retrospective rating plan, the buyer would be wise to consult an experienced insurance advisor or agent.

Ways to Control Costs

This chapter gives several ways to control retrospective rating plan costs or capture cash flow.

> **(BPF × standard premium) + (LCF × losses) + (excess loss premium) × tax multiplier = indicated retro premium**
>
> BPF = Basic Premium Factor—A percentage factor that, when multiplied by the standard premium (premium derived from manual rates), will provide a charge (the basic premium) for insurer profit, contingencies, and expenses (except for loss adjustment expenses). This is the "plus" part of the "cost plus" formula.
>
> LCF = Loss Conversion Factor—A percentage factor that, when added to 1.00 and then multiplied by the dollar value of losses, will provide a charge for both the losses and the loss adjustment expenses. Most of the "cost" part of the retrospective premium charge comes from this calculation.
>
> Excess Loss Premium—An excess loss premium is charged for limiting individual losses to a specified level to reduce the effect of unusually large losses on the final premium. The excess loss premium is calculated by this formula: standard premium times excess loss premium factor times LCF.
>
> Tax Multiplier—The tax multiplier reimburses the insurer for premium taxes paid to the state(s).
>
> Indicated Retro Premium—This is the amount of premium, subject to the minimum and maximum premium, that the insured must pay. The *minimum premium* is the lowest premium that will be charged, even if the formula results in a lower indicated retro premium. Likewise, the *maximum premium* is the highest premium that may be charged, even if the formula results in a higher indicated retro premium.

Figure 10.1. The retrospective rating formula.

80. Carefully Select Retrospective Minimum and Maximum Factors

To develop the net costs (insurer overhead and profit) under a retrospective rating plan, the standard premium is multiplied by a basic premium factor to develop a *basic premium*. The basic premium includes such items as insurance company expense, agent's commission, insurer profit, and an "insurance charge." The insurance charge allows the insurance company to fund for the possibility that some insureds will have losses that cause the indicated retrospective rating premium to exceed the maximum premium and are therefore not reimbursed to the insurer. As a result, the higher the maximum premium assumed by the insured, the lower the insurance charge. Concomitantly, the minimum premium amount also affects the insurance charge. For instance, the higher the minimum premium, the higher the likelihood that losses will fall below those that would produce the minimum premium and that the minimum premium will have to be paid by the insured. Thus, the minimum premium guarantees a certain level of premium income to the insurer. Therefore, the lower the minimum, the higher the insurance charge.

At some point in time, there is a point of diminishing returns. In fact, at some point the insurance charge actually disappears and any additional increases in the maximum or minimum will not depress the basic factor any further.

A reasonable set of factors for a 1-year plan is usually a 50 percent minimum and a 120 percent maximum. Many insureds will ask for a basic factor based on these minimums and maximums. A question along the following lines should then be asked, "Assuming a 50 percent minimum, at what maximum level will the insurance charge disappear?" If the answer is 1.40, i.e., a possible penalty of 40 percent, the buyer should avoid, if possible, assuming a maximum factor above 1.40 since no compensation will be received for assuming additional risk.

Some business managers are so attracted to the possibility of a very low minimum premium that they select it even though it would be virtually impossible for their organization to benefit from it. In other words, the amount spent by the insured to attain such a low minimum would not be offset by the payment of very low losses. Past loss experience should be considered when choosing a minimum premium. It is often a better deal to increase the minimum and lower the basic premium charge.

Another way to reduce the insurance charge is to assume a 3-year term plan. Under this approach, 3 years of premiums and losses are used in the calculation instead of 1 year's premiums and losses. As a result, an insured could conceivably have excellent experience for 2 years and 11 months and expect a large retrospective return only to have a string of severe losses occur during the 36th month, wiping out all of the returns for the past periods as well as creating an additional premium. The 2 or 3 percentage points reduction in the basic factor may not warrant this large exposure. In the event that a 3-year plan is assumed, *higher minimums* and *lower maximums* should be assumed. The higher minimum will recognize the fact that the law of averages will better operate under a 3-year plan while the lower maximum will reduce the possibility of your paying additional premiums.

81. Negotiate Agent's Commission
Outside Rating Plan

As discussed in Chapter 8, insurance buyers for midsized and large organizations are now negotiating commissions with agents. Besides allowing for tailored services for fees paid, this may also reduce certain overhead and reinsurance charges. Many overhead and reinsurance charges are determined as a percentage of premiums. A general rule of thumb is that these overhead charges will run 30 to 35 percent of premiums.

For instance, let's assume that retrospectively rated workers compensation premiums will be $500,000 and the commission rate will be 5 percent, developing a commission of $25,000. Rather than paying $500,000 directly to the insurance company, an alternative might be to pay $475,000 to the insurance company and $25,000 to the agent. Since the insurer will not be paying the agent's commission, the basic factor would be reduced by 5 percentage points. The net effect would be: (1) a lower basic factor being applied to a lower premium; (2) a lower loss limitation factor being applied to a lower premium; and (3) a premium tax rate being applied to a lower premium. In this example, the resulting savings would be approximately $7,500 to $8,750.

Some insurers will not allow the full credits as applied in the above example because they try to determine the dollars needed and back into the basic premium factor. In other words, they might reduce the basic premium factor by 2.5 to 3.0 percent instead of the full 5 percent paid to the agent. However, even this more conservative approach avoids paying premium taxes on the agent's commission and may, therefore, be worthwhile.

82. Negotiate Other Retrospective Rating Factors

Other retrospective rating factors may be modified through negotiated factors or dividends. The remaining factors that might be negotiated are:

- Loss limitation factors
- Loss conversion factors
- Tax multipliers

To avoid the scenario in which one major catastrophic loss adversely affects the entire retrospective program, a *loss limit* can be purchased limiting a particular loss to an agreed amount. For agreeing to limit this loss, the insurance company makes a premium charge. While most states have guidelines for what the charges should be, the insurance company may charge more or less based on its perception of the risk or its cost of reinsurance. As a result, this is often a key point of negotiation.

The *loss conversion factor* is the charge made by the insurance company for the adjustment of claims by its own staff and, in the case of workers compensation, outside legal counsel. Insurance companies will sometimes agree to reduce the loss conversion factor by 2 to 3 percentage points, as there is a hidden profit factor included in this charge.

The *tax multiplier* is supposed to reflect the amount of premium taxes paid to the state by the insurance company. However, insurance companies have methods of managing their state taxes in order to reduce them. Some insurance companies will pass along these state premium tax savings to insureds; this may be another important point of negotiation.

83. Explore a "Paid Loss" Retrospective Rating Plan

Under the retrospective rating plans discussed above, adjustments are made based on losses as valued 6 months after the end of the policy period and at 12-month intervals thereafter until all claims are closed. These "losses" include not only the amounts actually paid to claimants but also estimates of the amounts that will be paid in settlement of open claims. These estimated losses are called *loss reserves*. Well-managed insurers have a tendency to reserve conservatively in the hope that claims will close out lower than anticipated. However, this is not always the case. In any event, retrospective rating plans are adjusted annually—with settlements being made between the insured and the insurance company on any additional or return premiums. It may take as many as 10 years for all of 1 year's claims to be settled and paid. In the case of severe injuries under workers compensation, payments could go on for 40 or 50 years.

The timing difference between the date on which premiums are paid and the dates on which losses are actually paid is significant and usually results in substantial cash flow to the insurance company. Larger insureds, particularly those who pay more than $750,000 in premiums, have often successfully negotiated to share in the investment income on loss reserves. Perhaps the most common approach has been the *paid loss retro*. Rather than paying in premiums as earned, the insured simply reimburses the insurance company for its estimated expenses as well as actual paid losses during the first year. The balance of the loss fund is then paid to the insurance company over a period of time as the insurance company disburses such funds, thereby leaving the cash flow with the insured.

Under a paid loss retrospective rating arrangement, the insurance company assumes a much larger than normal financial risk in that it is responsible for the claims but has not collected the entire premium from the insured. As a result, the insurance company will normally require the insured to sign a premium note which is collateralized by a clean letter of credit or a special type of surety bond.

Many of these arrangements will terminate after 5 years and the insured will make a balloon payment, equal to any unpaid reserves, to the insurance company to "close out" that year's retro. While this plan leaves a substantial amount of cash with the insured until paid out in claims, some insurance companies will increase some of the retrospective rating factors to recoup their loss of the investment income. The increased rating factors can drive up the costs enough to eliminate the advantages of retaining the cash flow.

Paid loss retrospective rating plans are obviously a competitive tool and will be more available during soft markets than in tight ones. In addition, the larger the premiums paid by an insured, the stronger the insured's negotiating position.

Care should be taken in structuring these plans from a federal tax standpoint. The IRS is beginning to take the position that deferred premiums are not deductible business expenses until actually paid to the insurer. You should seek appropriate counsel when considering a paid loss retrospective rating plan.

84. Consider Other Cash Flow Programs

Other commonly used cash flow programs include the following:

- Negotiated deposits
- Deferred premiums
- Compensating balance plans
- Interest on reserves

Negotiated Deposits.   Many premiums, particularly those for workers compensation and general liability, are paid on a monthly or quarterly basis. Rather than accepting the creditworthiness of the insured, virtually all insurance companies require deposits to cover the period involved, i.e., the month or the quarter. For example, assume that premiums will be $10,000 per month. Most insurance companies will require a deposit of 20 to 25 percent of the annual premium, in this case $24,000 to $30,000. Typically, interest is not paid on these deposits, and the insured thereby suffers a loss of investment income. Some insureds have been successful in negotiating arrangements with a very low deposit premium (e.g., $500) using a clean letter of credit or appropriate surety bond as collateral for the additional amount owed to the insurer. If the insured can earn more on the invested money than the letter of credit or surety bond costs, a net savings is enjoyed.

Deferred Premiums. Many insureds have also been successful in negotiating a depressed premium payment arrangement. With this mechanism, the insured makes a low monthly payment during the policy
period and a balloon payment at the end to make up the difference.
Sticking with the previous example involving a $120,000 annual premi-
um, only $5,000 might be paid each month with the other $5,000 being
deferred until the end of the policy period. About 90 days after the end
of the policy period, a balloon payment of the $60,000 (12 monthly
payments at $5,000 each) is made. Generally, there is no required
collateral such as surety bonds or letters of credit.

Compensating Balance Plans. Many businesses negotiate annual lines
of credit with their banks. In return, they may be required to maintain
certain cash balances in non-interest-bearing accounts to support the
line of credit. For instance, the bank might require a compensating
balance equal to 10 percent of the overall line of credit as well as 10
percent of the average outstanding loan balance.

Let's assume that the insured has negotiated a $2 million line of credit
and expects to have a $1 million average loan balance during the year.
Based on a requirement of 10 percent of these two amounts, the insured
will be obliged to maintain a compensating balance of $300,000. Ar-
rangements could be made for the insurance company to collect the
premium and deposit it in a non-interest-bearing account at the insured's bank to maintain a bank balance of $300,000. Even though the
deposits are under the insurance company's name, the bank agrees to
allow these deposits to satisfy the insured's compensating balance
requirement. The insured can thus avoid tying up $300,000 in cash,
which could be used to reduce the average loan balance from $1 million
to $700,000, and can thereby attain an interest savings that is somewhat
higher than the short-term investment rate.

This approach is complex and difficult to negotiate because bankers
usually do not understand insurance and insurance underwriters often
do not understand banking arrangements. For insureds with high
compensating balance requirements, however, the results may justify the
effort.

Interest on Reserves. Perhaps the simplest way for insureds to benefit
from the cash flow on reserves is the interest on reserves concept. It
might be better described as a "now account" in the insurance arena. Just
as a bank keeps a record of all deposits and disbursements, the insurance
company would do the same for premiums and losses and would pay
interest on the balance of funds held. To simplify administration, most
insurance companies use ending or beginning balances rather than the

daily balances typically used by banks. In any event, the insurance company applies a mutually agreed-upon interest rate to the funds being held and remits the investment income, often as a "dividend," to the insured at an agreed-upon point in time.

When compared to a paid loss retro, interest on reserves avoids the complications, the financial risk to the insurance company, and the expense of letters of credit and/or surety bonds necessary with the paid loss retro. The interest-on-reserves concept might be particularly attractive to the insured that must collateralize the letter of credit used with a paid loss retro with the actual funds.

Some risk managers have described this approach as "cash value" casualty insurance. In any event, it is a simple method of sharing in the investment income otherwise enjoyed solely by the insurance company.

85. Examine the Self-Insurance/Captive Option

In the past, when the insurance market tightened and became noncompetitive, insurance companies increased rates while decreasing availability of cash flow alternatives. In addition, some types of insurance simply were not available during tight markets. This caused many insureds to consider and implement self-insurance programs.

A great deal of confusion arises over the terms noninsurance versus self-insurance. *Noninsurance* is the process whereby risk is assumed and no real records are kept of the final outcome. For instance, an auto garage does not insure against petty theft of its hand wrenches. Nor does it set up a reserve for such loss and carefully account for losses during a fiscal period. On the other hand, *self-insurance* is the formal assumption of risks and the accounting of results. Specific accounts or funds are set aside to fund the risks, and losses that do occur are charged against those accounts or funds. Not only does this process allow the business organization to proactively manage the risks involved, it also facilitates a reversion back to the regular insurance market if the insurance approach becomes desirable at some point in the future.

Self-insurance is used with those exposures where losses occur with enough frequency to make them predictable. This is often called the "working layer" or "burning layer." Potentially catastrophic losses should not be self-insured.

The area most often self-insured is physical damage to personal property such as automobiles and equipment. Many companies with large numbers of employees self-insure workers compensation and/or group health. As respects liability insurance, even the largest organizations must buy insurance at some level. Therefore, many will self-insure some first-dollar amount determined according to their ability to pay (e.g., $25,000, $250,000, $2,500,000) and purchase *excess liability* insurance above that amount.

As with retrospective rating plans, stop-loss insurance can be purchased so that no one catastrophic loss can impair the financial condition of the business. In addition *aggregate stop loss* may be purchased to limit the amount assumed when an unexpectedly large number of losses occur.

The advantages of self-insurance are numerous. They include greater financial rewards to insureds who control losses, potential cost reduction, increased cash flow, and more control over claims.

Disadvantages of self-insurance include delays in federal tax deductions until losses are actually paid, increased administrative costs, and the loss of a buffer between the employer and employee as respects self-insured workers compensation claims (i.e., the employee blames the employer for denying a workers compensation claim instead of blaming the insurer).

A natural extension to self-insurance is the formation of a *captive insurance* company. Generally, a captive is a funding vehicle used by sophisticated risk managers. Its primary purpose is to insure the risks of its parent or affiliates. Advantages of captives include more control over reinsurance placements, flexibility in arranging services such as claims and engineering, and formal handling of risks for which insurance is not available in the marketplace. Disadvantages include additional administrative costs and scrutiny by the Internal Revenue Service.

Any business paying over $500,000 in property and casualty premiums, excluding umbrella liability, should carefully review self-insurance, and any company paying in excess of $2 million should review the wholly owned captive approach.

86. Consider Group Self-Insurance/Captives

While the medium- to large-sized business organizations developed and used the self-insurance and captive concepts, the small- to medium-sized businesses have also desired the benefits. Many states fulfilled this desire by passing enabling legislation to allow qualified groups of employers to join together in self-insured trusts for workers compensation insurance, often called "workers compensation pools." Where legislative support to allow pools was not available, associations and other groups formed group captives. Association/group plans have met with varying degrees of success. Common problems have involved lack of adequate reinsurance, inadequate capital, and poor management.

However, group programs can work if the participants view them as a long-term approach to meeting their insurance needs and are willing to commit the appropriate time, capital, and resources to the project.

Group Captives. The tight markets experienced in 1976 to 1978 and 1984 to 1987 spawned numerous group and industry captives. Reasons for forming a group captive, as opposed to each organization's funding its own risks, include:

- Increased accuracy of statistical forecasts because of the volume of data (i.e., the law of large numbers)
- Better purchasing power as respects reinsurance and services
- Reduced overhead because fixed costs can be spread over more units
- Greater risk retention capabilities (financial muscle)
- The degree of risk transfer and distribution may make premiums deductible for tax purposes

Problems commonly associated with group captives include:

- Improper reserving of losses—since captive owners have a tendency to be overly optimistic
- Underestimation of development, start-up, and maintenance expenses
- Involvement of too many middlemen
- Use of inexperienced management
- Frequent heavy broker and insurance company resistance

The growth of group-owned captives, especially offshore captives, has been fueled by tax issues. Once membership exceeds 15, there is probably sufficient "spread of risk" to meet IRS guidelines and make premiums deductible business expenses. In addition, prior to the 1986 tax bill, if ownership was arranged in a certain manner between 9 or more nonrelated shareholders, profits would not be subject to U.S. income taxes until brought back to the United States. However, the 1986 tax law removed this tax-deferral benefit. As a result, most industry observers expect many offshore captives to relocate in the United States while most new captives will be formed in the United States.

Pools and Risk Retention Groups. On October 17, 1986, President Reagan signed the Liability Risk Retention Act of 1986. In effect, this broadened the Risk Retention Act of 1981, which allowed groups of businesses to pool their products liability risks with a minimal amount of interference from state insurance regulators. Products liability results from injuries or property damage caused by products manufactured by a business after the products are sold to consumers. Due to the soft market that ensued after 1981 and the narrow scope of coverages allowed under the original act, very few businesses took advantage of it. When the insurance crisis developed in 1984 to 1986, Congress decided to broaden the act to alleviate the new "crisis".

Under the new act, two or more businesses can now join together and pool any type of liability risks (excluding workers compensation and personal lines). In other words, automobile liability, general liability, umbrella liability, directors and officers liability, professional liability, and other liability coverages can be covered by a *risk retention group*. To start such an operation, a group must form an insurance company which is licensed in a state. Of course, some states require lower initial capitalization and impose fewer regulatory constraints than others, making them more favorable domiciles. Favorable domiciles currently include the states of Colorado, Delaware, Hawaii, Tennessee, and Vermont. The Risk Retention Act then requires the risk retention group to file a business plan in all other states in which it will operate; but it gives insurance commissioners very little authority to regulate risk retention groups that are not domiciled in their state.

Perhaps equally important, the Risk Retention Act also authorizes the establishment of *purchasing groups* which really do not assume any risk. They merely use the group's buying power to purchase insurance more economically on behalf of group members. In the past, associations have established "safety groups"; however, many states and insurance companies did not recognize these as legal organizations. The new legitimacy of purchasing groups will affect the entire marketing system of commercial insurance in the United States.

Overall, the Risk Retention Act may be the most significant piece of insurance legislation enacted in this country during the last 50 years, and it is expected to inject more competition into the insurance arena. A group or an association that forms an insurance purchasing group will be in a position to simply turn it into a risk retention group if the insurance industry fails to respond to the purchasing group's needs.

Risks Of Group Programs. While group self-insurance/pooling programs offer small and medium-sized organizations opportunities to enjoy the benefits of self-insurance, they also present new risks to their members. Since they are not significantly regulated and usually are not heavily capitalized, there may be a substantial risk of insolvency. There may also be substantial penalties for early withdrawal from these programs. Figure 10.2 lists some of the more important points that you should consider before joining a group/association captive, pool, or risk retention group.

The following are a few of the important questions that should be answered before one participates in any type of group insurance or self-insurance scheme.

· How and to what extent will it be capitalized?
· What will be the acceptable premium-to-surplus ratio, and how will this be controlled?
· How well could the facility handle multiple shock losses, and what would happen if it were financially incapable of handling adverse loss experience?
· At what levels, if any, will reinsurance be purchased?
· Who controls the facility, and are there conflicts of interest?
· Does the facility plan to work with the traditional insurance industry or compete against it?
· How is the facility viewed by the traditional insurance marketplace, and what reaction to participation, if any, is expected from insurers?
· Are there provisions for withdrawal of participants and the entry of new participants?
· Are there limitations and restrictions on the sale of the facility's stock by sponsors?
· What is the minimum required participation time, if any?
· How will premiums be determined?
· Are policyholders assessable, and to what extent?
· How are initial formation and ongoing operating expenses allocated to participants?
· How will any underwriting and investment income be distributed to participants?
· Is the coverage provided by the proposed policy form reasonable, or is it overly broad?
· Who will the other participants be, and are the risks to be insured homogeneous?
· What, if any, risk control efforts will the facility require of participants?
· Who will provide the claims adjusting and other necessary services, and how will the service provider be compensated?
· Are liquidation procedures spelled out in the plan documents?

Fig. 10.2. Group and association self-insurance pools and captives — some questions to ask. (*Source: Reprinted from* Risk Financing *with permission of the publisher, International Risk Management Institute, Inc., Dallas, Texas. Copyright 1986.*)

Summary

This chapter applies primarily to medium- and large-sized businesses. However, some of these points are for everyone, particularly those involving risk retention groups and insurance purchasing groups.

For insureds who wish to assume reasonable risks for profit, the assumption of insurable risk and the resulting savings provide an outstanding opportunity to reduce operating costs.

11
Insurance Bidding

Insurance bidding is a technique widely used for selecting an agent/broker and arranging an insurance program. The most common reasons for bidding an insurance program are to reduce premium costs, to improve coverages, and/or to select a new agent/broker or insurance company because of dissatisfaction with current services. In a buyers' market, the competitive bidding process may provide all of these benefits. In a tight insurance market, it may take competitive bidding even to procure insurance for the organization, or bidding may be necessary because the current insurance company decides to severely restrict coverage or substantially raise premiums.

Bidding Methods

There are a number of insurance bidding methods. The one selected depends largely upon the method to be used for selecting an agent/broker. The basic decision to be made is this: will a single producer be chosen to approach the insurance companies or will several producers be allowed to approach them? In either case, some preselection of producers will be needed unless there is a decision to remain with the current agent/broker. Requesting several agents/brokers and/or direct writers to quote on an account has many advantages including the following:

1. Maximizes competition between producers as well as between underwriters.

2. Maximizes the number of insurers approached, since different producers use different companies.

3. Involves direct writers as well as independent agents in the competitive bidding.

The disadvantages of using several producers/direct writers, rather than selecting a single one from whom to obtain quotations, include:

1. Use of a number of agents/brokers reduces the flexibility of each in picking the best combination of insurance companies.

2. Use of several agents/brokers means that excess and specialty lines cannot normally be bid because of the limited number of insurance markets and/or limited availability of reinsurance markets to provide them.

3. Use of a hired consultant may be required, since it is usually not good practice to allow one of the brokers to prepare specifications. Otherwise, management will have to take an active role in doing so.

The advantages of appointing a single producer to market the insurance are:

1. There is virtually no market disruption.

2. The producer is afforded maximum flexibility to select the appropriate combination of insurance companies.

3. The selected producer can be relied upon to prepare the specifications, subject to management review.

4. Underwriters may take more interest in the account because they know the producer will definitely write the business.

5. Specialty and excess coverages can be marketed along with the primary lines.

The disadvantages of appointing a single producer to market the insurance include:

1. There is less incentive for the producer to obtain the most competitive insurance program since the producer knows he or she will get the business.

2. Fewer insurance companies will probably be approached than when several producers are involved.

If a decision is made to consider agents/brokers or direct writers in addition to or in lieu of the current producer, some preselection is necessary. A number of producers and direct writers should be approached and requested to provide data regarding their qualifications to properly service the organization's insurance needs. This information should address the following: the number of years in business, the number of employees, the number of similar types of accounts, and résumés for the account executive and the assistant who will be working on the organization's insurance program. This process can involve as many insurance agents/brokers and or direct writers as desired. Once the information is received and an initial review is performed, some business managers will request each agent/broker to come in for an interview to discuss the firm's overall needs, how the agent/broker might handle the account, and the agent's/broker's qualifications. Based on this information, all but four or five agents/brokers and/or direct writers are eliminated from consideration. Two or three agents/brokers and two or three direct writers can then be used, or only one agent/broker can be chosen.

At this point, either a conceptual proposal or a competitive proposal can be requested. A *conceptual proposal* involves a specific explanation of how the agent/broker or direct writer would design the program. The proposal would include such things as a list of the insurance companies to be approached, an outline of recommended insurance coverages, modifications to standard policies that could probably be negotiated, an explanation of how the producer would be compensated, and a discussion of the services which would be available to the insured. In a review of the conceptual proposals, such things as innovation, thoroughness, knowledge of exposures common in the organization's industry, service capabilities, and communications ability of the producer should become evident.

Although practices vary, the conceptual proposal is generally utilized when there is a desire to select only a single producer to prepare specifications and approach the insurance marketplace. In any case, the field should be further pared down—following the conceptual proposals—to one, two, or perhaps three agents/brokers and/or direct writers. If a single organization is chosen, it is then requested to go out and put together the program it has suggested. If two or three organizations are to be used in the remainder of the process, they should be requested to go out and obtain competitive proposals.

Competitive proposals are utilized when more than one producer and/or direct writer are to be invited to bid on the organization's insurance or when a single producer is to obtain proposals from several insurance companies. This process involves the preparation of written insurance specifications which contain underwriting data and an outline of the desired insurance coverages for use by the producers or direct writers in preparing their proposals. If a single agent/broker has been selected to market the program, that producer can prepare the specifications and approach the markets chosen to quote on the firm's account. If, however, several producers/direct writers will quote on the account, insurance specifications must be prepared. When several producers are involved, it is normally best to avoid conflicts of interest by not allowing any one of them to prepare the specifications; however, their input and advice could be solicited. If the insured does not have the experience to prepare the specifications, some consideration might be given to hiring a consultant.

Ways to Reduce Costs

Five ways to increase the effectiveness of and cost savings associated with competitive bidding are presented in this chapter.

87. Don't Bid Too Frequently

Many organizations, particularly public entities, make the mistake of bidding their insurance too frequently. An organization which bids its insurance too frequently will quickly earn the reputation of being a "shopper," which will result in a diminishing amount of competition each time the insurance is bid and, eventually, in all agents/brokers and insurers in the community losing interest in the organization's account. This will lead to difficulties in finding insurance at all and, when it is available, in higher costs than are necessary. While it is difficult to generalize about frequency, an organization should probably not bid its insurance more than every 3 to 5 years unless unwarranted cancellations or rate increases occur.

88. Allocate Insurers to the Agents/Brokers

When several agents/brokers are used to bid competitively on the insurance program, a certain amount of control over the bidding process must be maintained. One key area to control is insurance markets selection. When it is not controlled, there will be a problem. A number of agents/brokers may approach the same insurance company to obtain proposals for the organization's account. Each underwriter, immediately recognizing that the insurance is being bid, will be forced either to select his or her "favorite" agent/broker (to whom the proposal will be given), to provide all agents/brokers with the same proposal, or to decline to bid on the account at all. Regardless of the approach taken by the underwriters, the effectiveness of the bidding process will be impaired.

To avoid this scenario, ask the agents/brokers who will be bidding on the account for a list of the insurance companies they want to use. The list should be prepared in order of priority and should indicate the premium volume that the agent/broker has with each company. If a national or large regional broker is being used, request the premium volume for that branch office only rather than for all of the brokerage's offices combined. When these lists are received, eliminate duplications— using the order of priority and the premium volume indication as criteria. In eliminating duplications, it is important not to split a company group between two or more agents. Keep in mind that many large insurers (e.g., Hartford Insurance Group, U.S. Insurance Group, CIGNA, The St. Paul Companies, and American International Group) actually may write coverage through several different companies. These sister companies will not bid against each other.

Advise all agents/brokers of the markets they may use and inform them that they will be disqualified from the bidding process if they approach any others. Additional markets may be requested by agents/brokers during the bidding process, and the agent/broker should be allowed to use them as long as they have not been allocated to a competing firm.

The use of market allocation will avoid the confusion in the marketplace that would result if several agents/brokers solicited proposals from the same insurance companies; it will also cause the agents/brokers to approach a large spread of insurance companies that might be interested in the account. The process is important and should be required of all bidders.

89. Allow Adequate Time to Secure Proposals

It can take a substantial amount of time to properly prepare a proposal for an insurance program. The amount of time required will depend upon the size and complexity of the account, the time of year in which the program will become effective, and the number of proposals that will be received. However, it will take between 3 and 5 months for most commercial accounts. In general, allow 30 to 60 days to preselect producers and prepare specifications, 30 to 90 days for the underwriters, and 30 days to evaluate the proposals and place coverage.

90. Provide Adequate Information

Probably the most common mistake made when obtaining competitive insurance bids is the failure to provide adequate data to the underwriters. Some insureds make the mistake of simply presenting copies of the current insurance policies to the various agents/brokers and direct writers who will be bidding on the account. This approach has the following major disadvantages:

1. Any coverage deficiencies or mistakes made by the current agent or company may be repeated in the new program.

2. Important underwriting and rating data will not be up to date.

3. The loss history of the firm is not disclosed.

4. The potential for obtaining broader and better coverages will be reduced if the producers are told to simply duplicate the current program.

5. The agent/broker may be biased by the current rates.

To avoid these mistakes, you should prepare written insurance specifications. While this does take time and effort, the results will be well worth it. The overriding consideration when designing insurance specifications is to achieve a total interchange of necessary underwriting information in a formalized manner.

The information included in specifications should consist of the company's operational and management history; plans for the future; coverage required and coverages desired; loss exposures faced; past loss history and detail of major losses (e.g., those over $5,000); and information regarding the organization's loss control and safety program. Figure 11.1 outlines the possible contents of a set of specifications. Those who desire information on what to include in insurance specifications can purchase International Risk Management Institute's *Guidelines for Insurance Specifications*. It provides business managers with a model set of specifications that can be tailored to the organization's individual needs.

In summary, the following data is of key importance to underwriters and should always be provided when an insurance program is bid competitively: at least 5 years of current loss information; detail on large losses; exposure base information (e.g., updated payrolls, sales, and property values); and information regarding the organization's safety and loss control program.

91. Don't Bid "Excess and Surplus Lines" Coverages among Agents

Certain types of insurance policies are written by such a limited number of insurance companies that it is a severe mistake to try to competitively

1. **Preface**—indicating coverages being bid, due date for quotes, whom to contact for additional data, and so forth

2. **Operations**—information regarding the management and operations of the firm

3. **Comprehensive automobile liability and physical damage coverage requests**—with an exhibit scheduling all owned vehicles, model, year, use, weights (GVW), and cost new

4. **Comprehensive general liability coverage requests**—with an exhibit providing rating information (e.g., classification codes, payrolls, receipts)

5. **Workers compensation coverage requests**—with an exhibit containing rating information (e.g., classification codes and payroll for each code)

6. **Contractor's equipment coverage requests**—including a schedule of equipment disclosing insurable values

7. **Crime insurance**—including the number of class A, B, and C employees and a brief description of internal controls

8. **Property (building and contents) insurance**—including a schedule of locations and values

9. **Loss history**—summary of total losses by year for all lines of coverage being bid

10. **Detailed description of losses**—over a specified amount

11. **Requested rating plans**—e.g., guaranteed cost, dividends, retrospective rating, cash flow enhancements, and so forth

12. **Information regarding the firm's risk management**

Figure 11.1. Insurance specifications outline.

bid them among a number of agents/brokers. Usually these types of policies are the ones obtained in the excess and surplus lines (E&S) insurance marketplace. In general, the E&S marketplace consists of insurance companies that write unregulated lines of specialized insurance. For example, Lloyd's of London operates in this marketplace. Typically, the types of insurance policies that fit into the category—and that should not be competitively bid among a number of agents/brokers—include errors and omissions, malpractice, and professional liability insurance. In addition, organizations seeking high dollar limits (i.e., over $5 million) of umbrella liability insurance should not attempt to obtain competitive proposals from more than one agent for the entire amount of coverage that they will need. When obtaining competitive proposals from several agents, request no more than $5 million in umbrella liability insurance.

In situations where professional liability or high limits of umbrella liability insurance will be needed, it is suggested that the agent or broker who wins on the other portions of the account be requested to obtain proposals from the markets that provide these coverages. Keep in mind that a single agent/broker can go out and obtain competitive proposals from several excess and surplus lines insurance companies. Therefore, even if one agent or broker is used for these lines of insurance, that agent/broker can canvass the market and present several proposals from various insurance companies from which the business manager may select.

12

General Recommendations

Today, many organizations spend more on insurance premiums than they do on income taxes. For this reason, the insurance cost center should be managed proactively just as is the income tax cost center. To manage an insurance program, the business manager does not necessarily have to be an expert on insurance and risk management. However, the business manager does need enough knowledge to ask the right questions and demand effective services. This knowledge can be obtained by reading industry technical publications and books and attending insurance industry-sponsored or trade association-sponsored insurance seminars.

Insurance Cycles

The property and casualty insurance industry is cyclical in nature. Table 12.1 shows a 12-year summary of premiums, losses, and net pretax financial results of the industry. Figure 12.1 shows the property and casualty insurance industry's net income after taxes for the years 1980 to 1986. Until 1981, the higher underwriting losses were offset by even higher investment income. Rocketing stock prices enhanced the investment earnings of insurance companies in 1982 and added to operating results in 1983. As can be seen, insurance industry underwriting losses were mounting during the early 1980s while investment income growth was slowing.

In 1984 and 1985, the bottom fell out. The year 1985 produced the worst operating results in the history of the industry.

Table 12.1 Recap of Operating Results for
U.S. Insurance Industry (In billions)

Year	Net written premiums	Underwriting profit/loss	Investment income	Pretax income
1974	32.1	3.8	1.2	
1975	48.1	(4.2)	4.1	.1
1976	58.7	(2.2)	4.8	2.6
1977	70.1	1.1	5.8	6.9
1978	79.1	1.3	7.3	8.6
1979	86.9	(1.3)	9.3	8.0
1980	96.4	(3.5)	11.2	7.5
1981	100.0	(6.5)	13.3	6.6
1982	104.4	(10.5)	15.1	4.2
1983	109.3	(13.4)	16.0	2.3
1984	118.6	(21.7)	17.7	(3.9)
1985	144.8	(24.9)	19.5	(5.6)
1986*	129.9	(12.3)	15.8	3.5

*Nine months.
SOURCE: Insurance Services Office, Inc., A. M. Best Co., Inc.

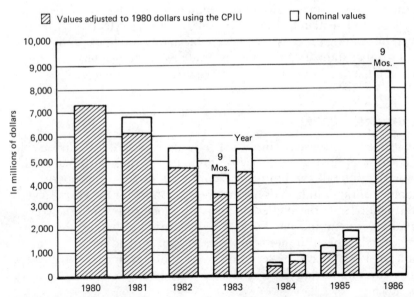

Figure 12.1. Net income after taxes. (*Source: Used with permission of Insurance Services Office, Inc.*)

Insurance companies drastically increased rates and premiums during 1985 and 1986. As can be seen, the industry was recovering in 1986. The authors believe that insurance companies will soon begin competing with each other once again, which will cause prices to stabilize and eventually begin to decline again. And the cycle will start over.

The purpose of this discussion is to point out that while insurance industry cycles are not totally predictable, changes can be anticipated. Business managers who proactively manage their insurance and risk management programs place themselves in a position to anticipate these changes; they take steps to take advantage of trends toward a "soft" insurance market and to protect their organizations from drastic upswings as the market begins to harden. Proactive management of an insurance and risk management program can be achieved by expending some time and effort in learning the basics of risk management and insurance and in following insurance industry developments.

Ways to Reduce Costs

This concluding chapter reviews 10 general techniques that can be used to reduce the premiums on all your insurance policies. These techniques either apply to several of the insurance policies purchased or are suggestions for risk management programs.

92. Consolidate Effective Dates

Among the tricks some insurance agents have used in the past to make it difficult for their clients to move to another agent is putting a different renewal date on every insurance policy. In other words, the various insurance policies (e.g., automobile, general liability, and property) expire on different days of the month and/or different months of the year. This makes it virtually impossible to obtain competitive insurance proposals on the entire program from other agents. It also makes it difficult to simply move the entire program to another agent with an "agent's letter of record." Furthermore, using different renewal days for the primary (e.g., auto and general liability) policies and the umbrella liability policy can cause gaps in insurance coverage.

For these reasons, it is advisable to arrange the insurance program so that a common renewal date(s) is used. For smaller organizations, it is probably best to use a single anniversary date for all policies. Larger organizations, however, may prefer two or three anniversary dates, to spread out over a period of time the work involved with renewals. For example, a large organization may use one date for all of its liability policies and another for all of its property insurance policies. Some organizations might even use a third common renewal date for all specialty and professional liability insurance policies. In addition to making it easier to competitively bid the insurance program, the use of one, two, or three common policy anniversary dates will allow the business manager to consolidate the gathering of renewal and underwriting information for the insurance companies.

It is strongly recommended that the business manager or risk manager avoid using January 1 or July 1 as the anniversary date for any of the insurance policies. January 1 concludes the busiest period of the year for the insurance industry. There are probably more insurance policy renewals effective on January 1 than on any other day of the year. In addition, many insurance companies renew their reinsurance treaties on January 1 and have difficulty committing themselves in advance of that date since they often do not know the terms of their reinsurance. July 1 is also a busy time of the year for insurance companies because, again, many reinsurance treaties are renewing at that time of the year. When the marketplace is changing, insurance companies are reluctant to quote terms far in advance of these reinsurance treaty renewals since they are not certain of their own costs for providing insurance.

For all but the largest firms, it is probably advisable to arrange the insurance program so that the policies renew in March, April, or early May. These months fall between the January 1 and July 1 busy periods of the insurance industry and avoid the summer vacation season. Except for the smallest organizations, the months September through December should probably be avoided because in "hard" insurance markets, insurers' capacity (the ability to write insurance or high limits of insurance) is often used up during the earlier months of the year and may not be available in the fall and early winter. However, smaller insureds will not generally be affected by capacity shortfalls unless they are for some reason purchasing very high limits (e.g., limits of over $50 million) of umbrella liability insurance or need a specialized professional liability policy (e.g., accountants, attorneys, and hospitals).

93. Maximize Purchasing Power with One Insurer

One touted advantage of the independent agency system over the exclusive agent or direct-writing insurance distribution system is that the independent agent has the ability to place an organization's insurance with more than one insurance company. Frequently, this approach can be used to maximize coverage and reduce costs. However, it is also possible to spread an insurance program too thin by using too many insurance companies for the various coverages. When this is done, the organization may not be considered an important account to any of the insurance companies which insure its risks. While this mistake happens most frequently when an organization uses numerous insurance agents, it can also happen when there is only one agent or broker. It behooves the insurance buyer to make sure that the organization is an important account to at least one of its insurance companies by placing enough policies (i.e., premiums) with that company to become an important account. By strengthening its position with the insurance company, the organization puts itself in a better position to negotiate on any claims for which an insurance policy's coverage is questionable. In the long run, this negotiating power in the claims area may be even more important than the ability to negotiate lower insurance premiums.

When thinking about this tactic of maximizing purchasing power with one insurer by giving that company a substantial amount of your premium volume, do not overlook the substantial premium dollars being spent on employee benefits (e.g., group health and accident) programs. Some insurance buyers have quite successfully used their group employee benefits programs as carrots to help obtain liability insurance that was otherwise unavailable in the marketplace or available only at an inordinate cost.

94. Buy Package Policies

This book has treated each line of insurance (e.g., automobile, general liability, and property) as a separate insurance policy. However, the insurance industry has developed some package policies which combine these various coverages into a single insurance policy for use by medium-sized and smaller insureds. For example, the extremely popular package called the Business Owners Policy (BOP) allows an insurance company to write general liability, property, and crime insurance in one policy. Insurance companies typically give a "package discount" in recognition of the reduced administrative costs of issuing a single policy rather than three separate ones. These discounts vary, but they generally range between 7 and 35 percent of the total premium.

95. Prepare or Verify Premium Audits

When certain policies, such as workers compensation, general liability, and automobile insurance, are first written, the premiums are usually based upon an estimate of what the actual exposure (e.g., sales, payroll, and number of vehicles) will be during the year. The actual earned premium for these policies is then usually determined after policy expiration by way of a premium audit performed by the insurance company. Because of the amount of these premiums, the year-end premium audit should be approached with the same degree of concern as the federal income tax return.

Business managers should work with the premium auditor to make sure that the information received is appropriate. Some business managers actually prepare the audit to be certain it is done properly.

Prepare It Yourself. At the beginning of the policy period, or a relationship with a new insurance company, a sample of the audit department's work sheets should be obtained. At the end of the year, the business manager or accounting department should develop the ratable payrolls, using the format of this work sheet. The insurance company's audit department will make an appointment. At the time of the appointment, the auditor should be furnished the prepared work sheet, along with the records from which the information was compiled. The auditor should be requested to immediately check the work sheet, and any changes that are to be made should be discussed before the auditor leaves your premises. If necessary, the insurance agent or consultant can be required to attend any meetings involving disputed classifications or procedures.

However, the auditor will usually accept the statistics compiled by the employer. In most cases, it is worthwhile to be as cooperative as possible with these auditors and avoid adversarial confrontations.

Verify the Auditor's Work. If the premium audit is not prepared internally, as suggested above, make sure that the premium auditor provides copies of the handwritten work sheets used in performing the audit before leaving your office. A typed audit and premium invoice or return premium will be mailed at a later date.

When the typed audit is received, it should be checked against the handwritten work sheet for transposition errors. It should also be ascertained that the correct experience modifier (if applicable) has been used and that all mathematics involved in determining the premium are correct. Finally, all rates utilized in determining the premium should be checked against the original insurance policy; any discrepancy should be explained by the insurance agent or broker.

The calculations in the premium audit can easily contain mistakes made by the insurance company, and these mistakes can raise the

insurance buyer's premium expense considerably. If the above suggestions are followed, the premium audit can usually be checked in a short
period of time.

96. Defer Premiums

The business manager may be able to negotiate payment of premiums
on a monthly or quarterly basis rather than paying a lump sum at the
beginning of the policy period. In fact, many insurers offer this payment
schedule without charging interest on the deferred amount. In turn, this
allows the insured to retain and invest or otherwise use the deferred
premium until it is due.

If the insurance company will not finance the premiums, consider the
specialty premium finance companies which charge interest at a rate
slightly higher than prime. Since these notes are secured by the
unearned premium of the policy being financed, the rates may be lower
than the insured's normal borrowing rate and, in any case, will allow the
insured to hold its normal credit resources in reserve.

97. Develop a Comprehensive
Data Base

The importance of accumulating risk management and insurance data
cannot be overemphasized. Indeed, it is probably best compared to the
importance of maintaining proper income tax documentation. Risk
management and insurance information can be used in negotiating with
insurance companies, evaluating loss control programs, analyzing appropriate deductible or retention levels, and auditing the cost compo-
nents of an insurance or risk management program. This data is also of
crucial importance when obtaining competitive bids. An accurate and
current risk management and insurance data base will save the insurance buyer considerable sums of money over the long run. In fact, this
information is so important that some organizations have expended
substantial sums of money to set up computerized "risk management
information systems."

The minimum standards for a risk management and insurance data
base, whether computerized or not, are:

- Premium audit statements for the past 5 to 6 years for each line of
  insurance audited

- Retrospective rating adjustment statements for the past 5 years for
  each applicable line

- Currently valued loss reports for each of the past 5 years for each line of insurance
- Copies of insurance policies including all endorsements
- Experience rating work sheets for the past 5 years for each experience rated line
- Current property schedule
- Current vehicle schedule
- Current equipment schedule
- Copies of important lease agreements, construction contracts, and other business contracts

98. Prepare Early for Renewals

The importance of timing and of allowing adequate time to obtain competitive proposals was emphasized in the previous chapter. Even when there is no intention of changing insurance companies, it is just as important to prepare early for renewals. The business manager should accumulate all of the important underwriting data that the insurance agent and underwriter will need well in advance (e.g., 90 to 120 days) of the renewal date. The insurance agent/broker should be pressured to provide the renewal quotation 2 to 3 weeks prior to the renewal date. This will allow time to negotiate with the underwriter regarding any unacceptable aspects of the renewal quote or even to obtain alternative quotes from other insurance carriers if the renewal quote is unacceptable.

As a word of caution here, however, an underwriter's quotation should not be "shopped" in the marketplace. Insurance buyers that do this will quickly establish a poor reputation in the underwriting community that will eventually cost them more than they gain from the activity. Never tell one underwriter the price quoted by another underwriter that has to be beat.

In a tight marketplace, underwriters will intentionally not provide the insurance agent/broker with a renewal quotation until the last minute. These underwriters are attempting to avoid having their renewal quotations shopped or to avoid providing the insurance buyer with the opportunity to obtain an alternative quotation should the renewal quotation be unacceptable. While pressure should be placed on the insurance agent/broker to obtain the renewal quotation well in advance of the renewal date, it should be recognized that failure to do so may not be the agent's or broker's fault.

99. Hire a Risk Manager

Medium-sized and large organizations should consider the possibility of hiring a full-time risk manager. Such an individual has knowledge of the insurance industry and the risk management process and can implement a cost-effective program. Particularly for medium-sized firms, it is often difficult to decide whether or not the expenses of hiring a full-time individual to administer a risk management program would be cost-justified. One risk management commentator, David Warren, CPCU, suggests using 10 percent of the sum of the insurance premiums and losses as a guideline for establishing the budget of a risk management department. In other words, 10 percent of the total cash flows with which the individual would be dealing might be a reasonable budget for the department. This same guideline might be used to determine when to hire a risk manager. If the costs of hiring a risk manager and establishing the department are equal to or less than 10 percent of the sum of insurance premiums and losses, it would probably be worthwhile to hire a risk manager. The theory underlying this rule of thumb is that a risk manager with specialized knowledge and expertise should be able to save the organization at least 10 percent more than an individual who does not have this specialized knowledge and expertise.

100. Implement Contractual Transfer Programs

The effective use of hold harmless clauses and insurance requirements in business contracts (e.g., leases and construction agreements) can reduce or eliminate the need for certain types of insurance and/or reduce insurance premiums. Losses that the organization would otherwise have to pay can be transferred to other parties in these contracts. In addition, these other parties can be required to purchase insurance to pay any losses experienced by the business manager's organization. For example, an organization that is leasing office space in a building might require the landlord to assume responsibility for purchasing insurance on that building and waiving the rights of its insurance carrier to subrogate (sue) the organization even if an employee of the organization was liable in starting the fire.

An organization which employs independent contractors should contractually require those contractors to purchase liability insurance and workers compensation insurance. The organization can otherwise be held legally liable to third parties for injuries or damage to their property caused by the independent contractor or even be liable to pay workers compensation benefits to injured employees of independent contractors. Because of this, the organization's liability and workers compensation insurance company will charge an additional premium for this additional loss exposure if the organization does not require these insurance coverages from their independent contractors and procure certificates of insurance from them showing that this insurance coverage is in place.

It is beyond the scope of this book to provide an in-depth discussion of the many uses of and pitfalls involved with contractual transfer of risk. However, you should be aware that others will attempt to pass their risks on to you in business contracts. You can reduce costs and control premiums by attempting to pass your risks to others. This is an area in which active participation from a knowledgeable attorney and a professional insurance agent or broker can be quite helpful.

101. Control Your Losses

As mentioned several times in this book, the main component of insurance premiums is losses. Over the long run, losses will consume 60 percent or more of your premium dollars. All business managers should also understand that the cost of accidents is substantially more than the amount paid by insurance companies. A considerable amount of uninsured cost is incurred by businesses from employee work stoppage, record keeping, accident investigation, and similar activities following accidents. Many loss control experts believe these hidden costs are two to three times higher than the identified and insured costs. Therefore, these hidden costs should be kept in mind when considering the implementation of a loss control program.

Two approaches are used to control losses: the engineering approach and the human factors approach. The *engineering approach* is that taken by the Occupational Safety and Health Act (OSHA); it seeks to avoid accidents and injuries by installing protective safeguards and other mechanical devices on equipment, in automobiles, etc. While many of these activities are quite important, many safety and loss control specialists now believe that the *human factors approach* is probably more effective. It attempts to convince employees that they can avoid injuries and accidents and tries to motivate them to do so. This approach involves training programs and activities to motivate employees to work safely. Truly effective loss control programs rely on a combination of these two approaches.

The most important key to establishing an effective loss control/safety program is commitment from upper management. Safety and loss control awareness must come from the top down. While it is beyond the scope of this book to go into this topic in more detail, business managers should recognize that efforts to control the organization's losses could, in the long run, provide more substantial premium savings than all of the other 100 cost control techniques combined!

Appendix A
Claims-Made Liability Insurance[1]

Claims-made liability insurance (a liability insurance policy which utilizes a claims-made coverage trigger) has been around for many years. However, until 1986 its use was limited primarily to various professional liability policies. Claims-made general and umbrella liability insurance is now being used by some insurers, and its use may become quite prevalent during the next hard market cycle.

This appendix reviews the claims-made concept as it is used with general liability and umbrella/excess liability insurance. It is not simply a study of the Insurance Services Office (ISO) standard CGL form; rather, many of the variations that appear in umbrella policies and nonstandard primary policies are also addressed.

Coverage Trigger

An insurance policy's "coverage trigger" is the provision that defines what event must occur while the policy is in force in order for the policy to apply to any resulting liability. In other words, the coverage trigger is the mechanism that determines which policy in a series of policies will respond to a particular loss event.

Historically, the insurance industry has used the date of the injury as the triggering event for general liability and umbrella liability insurance. This is known as an "occurrence" or "accident" coverage trigger. With

---

[1]This appendix is based largely on and contains many excerpts from a chapter with the same title in *Construction Risk Management*, published by International Risk Management Institute, Inc., used with permisson. Copyright © 1986.

an occurrence trigger, the insurance policy in effect at the time a covered bodily injury or property damage loss occurs responds to that loss regardless of when the insured learns about the occurrence or when a claim is filed against the insured. In other words, the insured is assured that liability insurance protection will be available for claims made at any time in the future if the bodily injury or property damage occurs during the policy period.

The occurrence coverage trigger works quite well for both the insured and insurer in most circumstances. However, when bodily injury or property damage occurs over a long period of time (e.g., asbestosis, cancer, silicosis), the injury or property damage cannot be pinned down to a particular date; therefore, it is impossible to identify the single insurance policy that should apply to the situation. As a result, some courts have held that all insurance policies in place from the time the injured party is first exposed to the injury-causing conditions through the date when the injury is diagnosed apply to the injured party's claim [see, for example, *Keene Corp. v. Insurance Company of North America*, 667 F.2d 1034 (DC Cir. 1981), cert. denied, 102 s Ct1644-4 (1982)]. In order to avoid this stacking of policy limits, the insurance industry has introduced claims-made general liability and umbrella/excess liability insurance.

When a policy has a claims-made coverage trigger, the policy is triggered when the claim is made against the insured rather than when the covered injury or property damage occurs. Figure A.1 illustrates the difference between claims-made and occurrence insurance. When liability insurance is written on a claims-made basis, it is important to have a policy in force when the claim for damages or injuries is made against the insured. Since a substantial amount of time can lapse between the occurrence of an injury or damage and the bringing of a claim, restrictions imposed in the insured's liability insurance program after

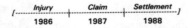

	Injury	*Claim*	*Settlement*	
[----	1986	1987	1988	----]

Assume Occurrence Policies:

The 1986 occurrence policy is triggered because the *injury* occurred during its policy period. The date of claim and settlement date have no bearing on which policy applies.

Assume Claims-Made Policies:

The 1987 claims-made policy is triggered because the *claim* was first made against the insured during its policy period. The date of injury and settlement date have no bearing on which policy applies.

Figure A.1. Illustration of basic and supplemental ERP. (source: *Reprinted from* Commercial Liability Insurance *with permission of the publisher, International Risk Management Institute, Inc. Copyright © 1986.*)

the occurrence of an injury or damage and prior to the bringing of a policy-triggering claim can cause gaps in coverage. The potential for such gaps because of the claims-made insurance mechanism has been extremely controversial. The remainder of this appendix addresses potential gaps in coverage related to the claims-made trigger, and the policy features that may be implemented to avoid them. Business managers should be certain they understand claims-made insurance and the particular features being incorporated into a policy before purchasing this type of coverage.

Retroactive Date

Unless modified, a claims-made policy covers any injury or damage that occurred in the past as long as the claim is made during the current policy period. This is often referred to as "prior acts" coverage. However, the insurer will normally want to limit the duration of prior acts coverage to avoid overlaps with previous occurrence policies, moral hazards associated with insuring future claims arising out of known past events, and to avoid covering claims that were previously reported to and investigated by another insurer. The underwriting tool that enables the insurer to limit the duration of coverage for prior acts is the "retroactive date" provision.

A *retroactive date* is simply a provision in a claims-made policy to exclude any claims that arise from injuries or damages that occurred prior to the retroactive date stated in the policy declarations. In other words, when a retroactive date is used in a claims-made policy, the insurer agrees to cover claims made during the policy period as long as the injury or damage for which the claim is made occurred on or after the retroactive date.

The imposition of a retroactive date is at the option of the underwriter. Ideally, an insured's claims-made policy will have no retroactive date, thus giving full coverage for claims made during the policy period regardless of when the damage or injury occurred. If an occurrence policy also covers a claim, the claims-made policy should apply as excess over the occurrence policy. However, most underwriters are likely to impose a retroactive date. If a retroactive date is used, it should be no later than the effective date of the first claims-made policy written for the insured, and the same retroactive date should be used for all subsequent claims-made policies. Once an insured has been covered under a claims-made liability policy, the advancement of its retroactive date will cause a gap in coverage. The gap will span the period of time between the original retroactive date and the new retroactive date.

As an example of how a coverage gap might occur due to advancement of a retroactive date, assume that an insured moved to a claims-made liability insurance program on January 1, 1986. The retroactive date for this policy is January 1, 1986, the date of the first claims-made policy. The expiring policy is then renewed on January 1, 1987, with another claims-made policy that contains a January 1, 1987, retroactive date. Without the implementation of some other policy provision to safeguard the insured, there would be no coverage for any claims made during 1987 involving injuries that occurred between January 1, 1986, and January 1, 1987. In other words, if a claim was made against the insured in 1987 that arose from an injury which occurred in 1986, there would be no insurance coverage for the claim. Fortunately, there are two types of safeguards that can be built into a claims-made policy (definition of "claim" and the extended reporting period) which reduce or eliminate this type of coverage gap. These policy safeguards will be discussed later.

Another way to reduce the possibility of coverage gaps occurring because of the advancement of a retroactive date is by requesting the underwriter to agree to stipulations specifying when the retroactive date may be advanced. Preferably, such an agreement will be outlined in the policy. However, even a separate letter or document is better than having no agreement whatsoever.

In conjunction with the 1986 commercial general liability (CGL) program, ISO implemented such stipulations as a rule (number 33) in its *Commercial Lines Manual*. The *Commercial Lines Manual* (CLM) contains the standard general liability rating rules and classifications. Summarized, this CLM rule specifies that the retroactive date may be advanced only when: (1) there is a change of insurers; (2) the insured fails to provide underwriting data that would be material to the insurer in writing the account or that is requested by the insurer; (3) there is a material change in hazard during the previous policy period; or (4) at the request of the insured. While these stipulations do not provide the insured with an ironclad safeguard against coverage gaps arising from advanced retroactive dates, this type of provision should reduce the frequency of abuses of the claims-made trigger. Nonstandard primary and umbrella liability policies usually contain no restrictions regarding the advancement of the retroactive date. However, many of these policies contain a stipulation in their "claims" definition that reduces or eliminates the underwriter's incentive to advance the retroactive date in order to escape providing coverage for a known loss event.

Definition of Claim

One key to claims-made insurance coverage is defining precisely when a claim is made. This definition can vary considerably from policy to policy. For example, the ISO claims-made CGL policy is triggered when the claim is "received and recorded" by the insured or insurer. Apparently, this means that the ISO policy would be triggered when the injured party requests compensation for injuries or damages in writing or verbally.

Some claims-made policies (particularly excess liability policies) specify that a claim is not deemed to have been made until written notice is received by the insured or insurer. Such a definition of "claim" will probably cause a later triggering of the claims-made policy than would occur under the ISO definition.

Fortunately, many of the umbrella policies that include a stipulation for "written notice" in the definition of "claim" contain another feature which will usually eliminate this type of problem, as well as provide the insured with a safeguard that reduces coverage gaps caused by advancement of the retroactive date. This provision specifies that the policy is also triggered when the insured reports an occurrence (also called a "circumstance" or "event that may lead to claims") to the insurer. In other words, this provision specifies that the policy will respond to any claims made in the future which arise from an occurrence of injury or damage that takes place after the retroactive date, provided the occurrence is reported to the insurer during the policy period. The provision, in effect, provides "tail coverage" for each known occurrence that is reported to the insurer in compliance with the policy's terms and conditions. It reduces or eliminates the underwriter's incentive to advance the retroactive date only to escape providing coverage for a known loss event. While some policies provide no time limitation on when written claims associated with a reported occurrence must be received by the insured or insurer for the policy to apply, most of them do have time limitations (e.g., 3 or 5 years after the circumstance was reported). In other words, these policies stipulate that they will provide coverage for claims made within 3 to 5 years after termination of the policy if those claims arise from occurrences which took place after the retroactive date and were reported to the insurer during the policy period. If the claims are made by the injured party after the stipulated period of time has lapsed, the policy would not cover them.

Extended Reporting Period

As already noted, a claims-made policy only insures against claims made while the policy is in force. Since there is always a possibility that injuries have occurred but claims have not been made, this aspect of claims-made insurance can present substantial coverage gaps for an insured in certain circumstances. For example, each of the following incidents could result in some gap in coverage:

- The insurer cancels or refuses to renew a claims-made policy and the insured cannot buy a replacement.
- The insured cancels or does not renew and chooses not to buy a replacement policy.
- The insured switches from a claims-made policy to an occurrence policy.
- A claims-made policy is renewed subject to an advanced retroactive date.
- The insurer attaches an exclusion for a product, accident, or location to a renewal claims-made policy.

An extended reporting period (ERP) provision is the most common type of safeguard against these types of coverage gaps. In general, an ERP causes the policy to respond to claims made after the policy is terminated (i.e., canceled or nonrenewed) if the injury or damage for which the claims are made took place on or after the retroactive date and on or before the effective date of termination. The ERP may apply only as regards claims associated with the occurrences or accidents of which the insured had no knowledge (e.g., incurred but not reported) at the time the policy terminated, only to claims associated with occurrences or accidents of which the insured did have knowledge, or to claims arising from both known or unknown occurrences.

The ERP may or may not have a limit to its duration. For example, the ISO claims-made CGL form has both types. It's two "basic extended reporting periods," which apply automatically for no additional charge for virtually any circumstance where the insured may need them, are limited to 60 days and 5 years respectively. The "60-day mini-tail" automatically applies to claims made within 60 days of policy termination associated with occurrences of which the insured had no knowledge prior to the date of policy termination. The automatic 5-year extended reporting period applies to claims made within 5 years of the policy termination date if the occurrence of injury or damage took place and was reported to the insurer on or after its retroactive date and on or before the effective date of policy termination. The "supplemental extended reporting period," available at the option of the insured for an additional charge, has no limit to its duration and applies to claims associated with both known and unknown occurrences that are not covered by the two "basic extended reporting periods." In other words, the supplemental ERP covers:

1. Claims arising from known occurrences that took place and are reported on or after the retroactive date and before the date of termination, when the claims are made more than 5 years after policy termination

2. Claims arising from unknown occurrences that took place on or after the retroactive date and before the policy's date of termination, when the claims are made more than 60 days after policy termination.

In essence, the use of the supplemental extended reporting period option converts the claims-made program to an occurrence trigger for the period of time between the retroactive date and the policy termination date. See Figure A.2 , for a graphic illustration of how the basic and supplemental extended reporting periods in the ISO CGL fit together.

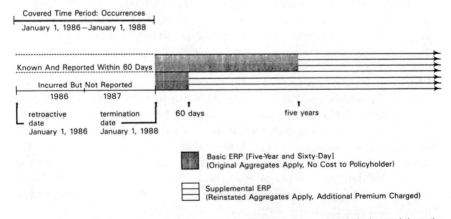

Covered Time Period: Occurrences
January 1, 1986—January 1, 1988

Known And Reported Within 60 Days

Incurred But Not Reported
1986   1987

retroactive   termination   60 days   five years
date   date
January 1, 1986   January 1, 1988

Basic ERP [Five-Year and Sixty-Day]
(Original Aggregates Apply, No Cost to Policyholder)

Supplemental ERP
(Reinstated Aggregates Apply, Additional Premium Charged)

As you can see in this illustration, the supplemental extended reporting period picks up where the basic extended reporting period leaves off. It covers claims first made after five years that stem from occurrences which were known and reported to the insurer within sixty days of the policy's termination. It covers claims first made more than sixty-days after policy termination that stem from occurrences of which the insured was unaware and therefore did not report to the insurer. The remaining original policy aggregates apply to claims covered by the basic extended reporting period. The supplemental ERP applies a separate set of aggregates, equal to the original policy aggregates, to claims it covers.

Figure A.2. Illustration of how the ISO CGL extended reporting periods operate. (SOURCE: Reprinted from Commerical Liability Insurance with permission of the publisher, International Risk Management Institute Inc., Copyright 1986.)

Nonstandard Extended Reporting Periods

For the most part, the ERP provisions we have seen in the nonstandard primary policies and umbrella policies are not as generous as those found in the ISO program. With regard to coverage for claims arising from an occurrence that took place and was reported to the insurer on or after the retroactive date and before the termination date, many policies provide coverage similar to that provided by ISO's automatic 5-year extended reporting period. This is accomplished by including a "notice of circumstance" provision in the definition of "claim" as discussed earlier in this section. However, many such policies place a 3-year rather than a 5-year time limit on this ERP. Some policies provide no time limit, thereby providing coverage similar to ISO's supplemental ERP as respects coverage for claims arising from known/reported occurrences.

With regard to coverage for future claims associated with occurrences that were incurred during the policy period but unknown to the insured and, therefore, not reported to the insurer, many nonstandard policies impose time limitations (e.g., 1, 3, or 5 years) on the extended reporting periods offered. For many insureds, particularly manufacturers and contractors, this type of tail coverage will prove to be of insufficient duration.

When reviewing a claims-made policy, the availability of the extended reporting period should also be carefully reviewed. Virtually all claims-made policies make extended reporting periods available in the event that the insurance company cancels coverage or refuses to renew the policy. While the ISO CGL form also guarantees the availability of an ERP if the insured cancels coverage or decides not to renew, many of the nonstandard policy forms do not contain this provision. Needless to say, the inability of the insured to purchase an ERP after deciding not to renew with his current insurer substantially decreases the flexibility of the insured to change insurers. It should also be determined if the ERP will be available in the event that the insurance company advances the retroactive date or attaches an exclusion on a renewal as respects claims arising out of specific products, accidents, or locations of the insured; a number of nonstandard forms are silent on these issues.

The cost or method of computing the premium, if any, for the ERP should be specified in the policy. For example, the ISO claims-made CGL provides the 60-day mini-tail and the automatic 5-year ERP for no additional charge and guarantees a maximum cost of 200 percent of the policy premium for the supplemental ERP. Some nonstandard CGL and umbrella policies indicate that an additional premium will be charged but do not specify how it will be calculated or place a limitation on its amount. Some umbrella liability policies do not specify that any additional charge will be made, but these tend to be the policies which are very restrictive in both the duration and availability of the extended reporting period.

It is also important to determine if purchasing the extended reporting period will reinstate the policy's aggregate limits of liability. The ISO claims-made CGL does provide for reinstatement of the aggregate limits when the supplemental ERP is purchased. When a claim is covered by the ISO form's basic extended reporting period, the original policy aggregate limits (less any reductions by paid claims) apply. Most of the nonstandard forms do not provide for reinstated aggregate limits when an ERP is purchased. Usually, any claims covered by their extended reporting periods will be subject to the policy limits remaining when the ERP is purchased. Needless to say, business managers should carefully compare the benefits of buying an ERP that offers only the remaining policy limits to the amount of the additional premium when making their decision to purchase the ERP.

Claims-Made Exclusions

Since a claims-made policy covers claims for injuries or damages that happened in the past but have not previously been reported as "claims," insurers are provided with the ability, and often the necessity, of making underwriting decisions after losses have occurred but before claims have been made. Claims-made exclusions can be incorporated into the basic policy or added to a renewal policy by endorsement to effect these underwriting decisions. One of the most important types of claims-made exclusions is the "exclusion of specific accidents" or the "exclusion of previously reported accidents."

An *exclusion of specific accidents* essentially advances the retroactive date as regards claims associated with known circumstances or accidents. When coupled with an extended reporting period applicable to the excluded accident or a definition of "claim" that includes claims arising from known circumstances which are reported to the insurer, the specific accident exclusion allows the underwriter to confine coverage for all claims arising from a known accident or event to a single policy and, consequently, a single set of the policy limits. The effect is similar to what would occur under an occurrence policy; the policy in place when the injury or damage is discovered by the insured and reported to the insurer will cover any claims eventually made for the injury or damage.

To illustrate how a specific accident exclusion would apply to a single accident, assume that 1 month prior to renewal of a contractor's claims-made liability policy, a major catastrophe occurs at a construction site resulting in substantial injuries and property damage. A number of claims are made during the 30-day period between the time of the catastrophe and the expiration of the policy in effect when the catastrophe occurs, thus triggering that policy for those claims. However, it is believed that several more claims will be forthcoming in the future. If the underwriter simply renewed the contractor's claims-made policy, the additional claims would be made against the contractor after the renewal policy had been put in place. The renewal policy would then be triggered for these new claims. Therefore, the contractor would benefit from coverage in two sets of limits of liability by triggering both of these claims-made policies.

To avoid having two claims-made policies triggered, the underwriter could advance the retroactive date of the renewal policy to the renewal policy's effective date. The contractor's expiring policy would then provide coverage (via the extended reporting period or a definition of "claim" that included a "reported circumstance") for all claims made in the future that arose from injuries that occurred and were reported to the insurer prior to the expiration date of that claims-made policy, including all claims which resulted from the catastrophe. The contractor would also generally have an opportunity to purchase an extended reporting period to cover any claims made in the future arising from events not previously known about or reported to the insurer. However, this approach would not benefit the contractor because additional premiums would be incurred for the optional ERP, and the claims made against it resulting from the catastrophe could very well exhaust its limits of liability. In such a case, the contractor would be left with no coverage for its future claims arising from occurrences that took place before the renewal policy's retroactive date, whether related to the catastrophic loss event or not.

A specific accident exclusion provides the underwriter with another option. It allows coverage for all claims arising from the catastrophe to be confined to the expiring claims-made policy, while still providing retroactive ("prior acts") liability coverage for any claims made against the contractor during the policy period of the renewal policy that resulted from occurrences not related to the catastrophe (i.e., true incurred but not reported accidents). In essence, a specific accident exclusion allows the underwriter to advance the retroactive date to the effective date of the renewal policy only as respects claims arising from the catastrophe. Depending upon the circumstances and the policy terms, the policy in place when the catastrophe occurred, the one in place when the catastrophe was reported to the insurer, or the policy that immediately precedes the first policy containing the exclusion would then be called upon to cover all claims arising from the excluded accident by way of an extended reporting period or the "notice of circumstance" claim provision.

A specific accident exclusion may be attached to an ISO CGL policy by endorsement. Many of the nonstandard claims-made liability policies that include "notice of circumstance" as a claim made contain such an exclusion within the policy form itself.

In a similar vein, the attachment of an exclusion for a specific product, work, or location precludes coverage for claims made during the policy period associated with both future and past injuries. For example, an underwriter might attach this type of exclusion when a particular project, product, or location presents hazards which the underwriter is unwilling to insure. Claims made for occurrences that took place in prior policy years (regardless of whether they are known or incurred but not reported) should be covered by an extended reporting period (or the prior policies if they are on an occurrence basis). This will probably involve the payment of additional premiums and may still create coverage gaps if the duration of the extended reporting period is limited.

Of course, an extended reporting period will not provide coverage for claims made in the future that are associated with injuries or damages which take place after the termination date of the policy to which it is applicable. For example, assume that a specific product exclusion is attached to a manufacturer's January 1, 1988, renewal, and the manufacturer buys the extended reporting period in the January 1, 1987, policy. The January 1, 1987, policy will insure any claims associated with injuries resulting from the products that occurred before January 1, 1988 (as long as they also occurred after the retroactive date of the January 1, 1987, policy). However, neither the January 1, 1987, policy nor the January 1, 1988, policy will cover product-related claims made after January 1, 1988, if the injuries for which they are made occurred after January 1, 1988.

Summary and Conclusion

While there is nothing inherently evil about claims-made insurance, a claims-made liability program does require knowledge, foresight, and coordination from the underwriter, agent/broker, and insurance buyer or risk manager. With occurrence insurance, safeguards are inherently built into the form such that a mistake on the part of any of these parties will not usually cause a coverage trigger-related gap in insurance protection. With claims-made insurance, however, a mistake or a malicious action on the part of any of these parties can cause a very serious trigger-related gap in coverage.

If there will be a "standard" claims-made liability insurance policy, it will probably be the Insurance Services Office commercial general liability (CGL) form. Particularly as respects the umbrella/excess liability insurance marketplace, there will be many variations from the ISO policy form provisions. While there will be exceptions, it currently appears that the ISO form, when taken as a whole, will provide insureds with the most safeguards against insurer abuse of the claims-made trigger. Prior to purchasing any claims-made policy, it will be important to determine the retroactive date that will be used, the definition of "claim," and the application, availability, duration, and cost of the policy's extended reporting period(s). The failure to review these provisions may very well result in significant insurance coverage gaps.

Ten Important Coverage Considerations

Although this book has concentrated on ways of controlling property and casualty insurance costs, the business manager should not fall into the trap of focusing solely on premiums while ignoring coverage. After all, the reason you buy insurance is to make sure that your organization is not financially impaired by fortuitous losses. This appendix discusses a few of the more important coverage issues that should be addressed by the business manager.

1. Coordinate Liability Policies

An organization's automobile liability, employers liability, general liability, and umbrella liability insurance policies must be arranged to coordinate with each other in order to avoid coverage gaps and overlaps. Not only must these insurance policies be reviewed individually, but consideration must be given to how they may interrelate to each other on a single loss event. Too many agents, brokers, and business managers fail to consider the possibility of a liability loss "falling through the crack."

Automobile and General Liability Coordination. An area in which disputes may arise with insurers is the distinction between an automobile-related claim and one that should be covered by the general liability policy. While the insurance industry has made attempts to clarify the distinction within policy contracts, there is still room for disputes when a liability loss involves the loading or unloading of a vehicle. In this situation, the automobile insurance company may claim that it is a general liability loss and the general liability insurance carrier may claim that it is an automobile liability loss. Frequently, the insured is left with no coverage (or a poorly coordinated defense) while the two insurance companies fight it out. For this reason, it is strongly recommended that the same insurance company be used for both the automobile and the general liability insurance.

A problem can arise even if the same insurer writes both the automobile and general liability insurance when one plan is subject to retrospective rating and the other coverage is not or when the two policies have different limits of liability. In these situations, the insurance company has an incentive to push the loss into whichever policy is on the loss sensitive rating plan or has the lowest limits of liability. In most situations, this will not be a problem, but organizations with a heavy auto exposure should probably consider using the same limits of liability and same rating plan for both types of insurance.

Coordinate Coverage Triggers.   As discussed in the previous appendix, another area in which policies must be coordinated is coverage triggers. Mixing coverage triggers in a layered liability program can result in gaps in coverage where one policy will cover liability losses but the one below or above it does not. When claims-made policies are purchased, an attempt should be made to coordinate the various provisions affecting the claims-made trigger. Generally speaking, it will also be preferable to use the most liberal policy forms in the lower layers of coverage, relegating the ones that provide you with the fewest safeguards to the upper layers which are less likely to be needed in the future.

Coordinate Primary and Umbrella Coverage.   The primary (general liability, auto liability, and employers liability) insurance policies must also coordinate with the umbrella liability program which provides the excess limits for catastrophe losses. To the extent possible, the umbrella should provide at least the same coverage (e.g., have the same exclusions, conditions, etc.) as the underlying policies. Of course, it is preferable for the umbrella to provide even broader coverage. However, areas in which umbrella policies are frequently more restrictive than primary policies include: coverage for pollution, coverage for damage to the work of an insured contractor, coverage for liability arising from aircraft and watercraft, and coverage for certain contractually assumed liabilities. Of course, there can also be other areas in which the excess or umbrella liability program is more restrictive than the underlying coverage. As a general rule here, any time the underlying coverage is enhanced by a policy endorsement, there may be a need to add a similar endorsement to the umbrella liability policy.

Another equally important area in which the primary and umbrella/excess liability policies must be coordinated is the limits of liability provision. Since an umbrella policy is intended to begin providing coverage once the primary policy has paid out its limits, it is important for the "Schedule of Underlying Limits" in the umbrella policy to accurately reflect the actual underlying limits purchased. For example, if the underlying limits are actually lower than those reflected in the umbrella policy schedule, the umbrella insurer will argue that it is not required to pay until the insured has made up the difference between the limits shown in the umbrella's schedule and the actual limits purchased. It is amazing how often mistakes are made in this area.

Another, more subtle, way that underlying policy limits can be lower than those required by the umbrella occurs when different inception dates are used for the primary and umbrella liability policies. Most umbrella policies require that the full aggregate limits of the primary policies be in force as of the inception date of the umbrella. If the primary insurance has an inception date earlier than that of the umbrella, any claims paid out by the primary carrier prior to the inception date of the umbrella reduce the primary policy's aggregate limits, causing a violation of this umbrella policy warranty. The resulting coverage gap is easily avoided by simply using the same inception and expiration dates for the primary liability insurance and the umbrella liability policies. Again, however, it is absolutely amazing how often this basic rule of thumb is violated.

2. Beware of Joint Venture Liability

Joint ventures are becoming a common way of doing business. They are frequently used by two or more manufacturers, contractors, real estate developers, or other business entities to combine their property, labor, skill, experience, or time, or some combination thereof, for a single undertaking. Whenever an organization enters into a joint venture, a new, distinct legal entity is formed. However, its liability exposures are not usually confined to the joint venture; the joint venturers usually have joint and several liability for the entity's actions. Unless proper steps are taken to insure this legal entity, the organization becomes exposed to potential uninsured liability losses.

The organization's liability insurance policies will not typically provide automatic coverage for liability arising out of past or current joint ventures unless specific modifications are made to the policy or the joint venture is scheduled in the policy as an "insured." It is usually preferable to arrange a separate insurance program to cover liability arising from the operations, products, and/or services of an active, ongoing joint venture, including the joint venture partners as insureds in the policies. Sometimes, however, one organization will simply endorse the joint venture and the partner(s) as insureds in its insurance program to provide coverage; this is most common when one of the partners supplies only capital and remains relatively silent in the operations and management of the joint venture.

It should also be recognized that there is a legal liability loss exposure arising from the products and completed operations of past, dissolved joint ventures. This is the area in which uninsured liability losses are most likely to arise since former legal entities are often forgotten. In addition, of course, specific liability insurance policies are not purchased for these dissolved legal entities. The business manager should make sure that any such loss exposure faced by the organization is covered by the liability insurance program.

3. Schedule All Insureds, Comply with Additional Insured Requirements

Another basic area that should not be overlooked is inclusion of all related entities as insureds in the various insurance policies. It is not at all uncommon for one or more subsidiaries or related organizations to be omitted from the schedule of insureds. One method of avoiding such an omission is to negotiate an omnibus named insured clause with the insurance company. In general, this endorsement would stipulate that all entities in which the primary named insured owns a majority interest are automatically included as insureds in the insurance policies. If such an omnibus clause is not obtainable, great care should be taken in reviewing the schedule of insureds to ascertain that none have inadvertently been omitted.

Don't Overlook Additional Insured Requirements. A similar problem can arise in regard to the inclusion of "additional insureds" on liability policies. It has become common practice for one party to a contract to require the other party to include it as an "additional insured" on the other party's insurance policies. For example, owners of construction projects will frequently require the general contractor to name the owner as an additional insured in the contractor's general liability policy. Without specific modification of the policy to provide automatic coverage in these situations, this can be achieved only by adding an endorsement to the policy specifically naming the additional insured. Frequently, contractors and others forget to request this endorsement, which could result in a breach of contract claim against the party that was supposed to take the action.

4. Report Acquisitions

Usually, liability insurance policies provide 60 or 90 days of automatic coverage for newly acquired or newly created organizations owned by the insured. The insured must report the acquisition or formation of a new company to the insurance company during this period of time to arrange for coverage after this time period has elapsed.

Consider the Implications in Advance. Many organizations make the mistake of not considering in advance the risk management implications of a merger, acquisition, or newly formed organization. After the fact, they often learn they have assumed uninsurable liability exposures or operations that are extremely costly to insure. Whenever possible, have the risk manager, agent, or broker make an analysis of the risk management implications of the deal before it is executed.

5. Promptly Report Potential Claims

Virtually all insurance policies contain a requirement to report accidents or occurrences which may result in a claim(s) "as soon as practicable." Failure to promptly notify the insurance company of known events that present the potential for liability claims can result in no coverage applying to claims that are eventually made in conjunction with the incident. Prompt reporting of accidents provides the insurance company with an opportunity to investigate the situation and receive statements from witnesses while memories are fresh. This puts the insurer in a better position to defend any claims that are eventually made. In the area of property insurance, insurance companies usually prefer to be advised of the loss and provided the opportunity to investigate prior to the commencement of major cleanup or repair operations. This enables them to also make an early determination of whether or not the loss event is covered by the insurance policy.

All organizations should put in place an incident reporting system whereby all accidents and events that may lead to insurance claims are promptly reported to the business manager with responsibility for the risk management and insurance program. It is also recommended that an attempt be made to secure an endorsement to liability insurance policies clarifying that the knowledge of an employee or agent of the insured does not constitute knowledge of the insured that a loss event has occurred for the purpose of reporting the accident. Knowledge would be imputed only when the individual is a corporate officer. This clarification will help avoid the potential for coverage denials based on late reporting when an employee knew about the accident but did not report it to management, thereby making it impossible to notify the insurance company.

6. Extend Notice of Cancellation

Most insurance policies require the insurance company to provide the insured with either 10 or 30 days' notice of its intent to cancel coverage. Insurance policies make no notification requirement on the insurer of its intent to not renew a policy or to substantially change a policy when it is renewed. For most commercial accounts, 30 days is an inadequate amount of time to remarket most insurance policies, and it is virtually impossible to do in 10 days. To avoid this scenario, business managers should request that the cancellation provision be modified to require the insurance company to provide at least 60 days' notice of its intent to cancel, and some companies will even agree to provide 90 days' notice.

In addition, the cancellation provision should be modified to address the issues of nonrenewal and material policy changes. An insurance company should be required to provide the same amount of previous notice (e.g., 60 or 90 days) of its intent to not renew coverage or to make a material change (e.g., including additional exclusions, advancing a retroactive date, or requiring substantially higher deductibles) when the policy is renewed. This type of policy modification is usually relatively easy to obtain in a soft, buyer's market and provides the insured protection when the market changes to a tight, seller's market. While more difficult to obtain in a tight market, it is often available in a tight market to medium-sized and larger commercial accounts.

7. Buy Adequate Policy Limits

A basic area of insurance management that deserves more attention than many business managers give it is the selection of policy limits. More uninsured losses probably are caused by improper selection of limits than by any other mistake.

Liability Limits.   One way of controlling insurance costs in a tight marketplace is to reduce the limits of liability applicable to the liability insurance policies you purchase. To the extent that the organization buys higher limits than it needs in a soft marketplace because of reduced premium costs, it is appropriate to reduce the limits applicable to the umbrella/excess liability policies it purchases in a tight market. However, the overriding concern of the business manager should be to protect the organization from catastrophic losses that, though they occur very infrequently, can substantially impair the financial position of the organization. Business managers should always keep in mind that it is better to assume risk at the lower levels through deductibles or self-insured retentions than in the high limits areas.

Most insurance and risk management professionals agree that the absolute minimum liability insurance virtually any business organization should purchase is $5 million. Of course, many organizations will need even higher limits. Cost reduction point number 43 in Chapter 4 contains additional guidelines on how to select an appropriate limit of liability.

Adequate Property Values. Business managers should also devote time and effort to making certain that the property values used for insurance purposes are adequate. Many insurance policies include a *coinsurance provision* which requires an insured to maintain insurance greater than or equal to a specified percent of the property's value (generally between 80 and 100 percent); failing to do so causes the insured to become a coinsurer with the insurance company and receive a reduced payment in the event of a loss. The purpose of a coinsurance clause is to promote "insurance to value" by penalizing the insured if proper values are not carried. The following formula determines the amount of the loss the insurer will pay:

$$\frac{\text{Value insured}}{\text{Value required}} \times \text{loss} = \text{recovery}$$

The value required is determined by the value of the property *at the time of the loss*, multiplied by the applicable coinsurance percentage. For example, assume a business owns a building that has an insurable value of $250,000 and insures it with a policy that contains an 80 percent coinsurance clause. The business would be required to insure the building for at least $200,000 ($250,000 × .80) to avoid a coinsurance penalty. If the business purchases only $150,000 coverage and sustains a $50,000 loss during the policy period, the recovery is limited to $37,500, less any deductible. The formula would be applied as follows:

$$\frac{\$150,000}{\$200,000} \times \$50,000 = \$37,500$$

Maintaining insurance to value is very important. Property should be appraised periodically to ensure that the amount of insurance carried is adequate. Another technique for avoiding coinsurance penalties is to purchase insurance on an *agreed amount* basis. Under this approach, property values for insurance purposes are determined and submitted to the insurance company. The insurance company reviews these property values and agrees that they will be adequate for insurance purposes. In essence, the insurance company will waive the right to apply a coinsurance penalty at the time of a loss even if these values turn out to be less than the stipulated percentage.

As a word of caution, agreed amount endorsements are generally on an annual basis even when attached to a policy with a 3-year term. Therefore, the property values usually must be reviewed and the agreed amount endorsement renewed annually. When 3-year term policies are purchased, this necessity is sometimes overlooked, which could result in a coinsurance penalty if a loss occurred in the 2d or 3d year.

8. Proper Property Valuation Clause

Under standard property insurance policies, the business is reimbursed for property losses on an *actual cash value* (ACV) basis. Valuation on an ACV basis is defined as the cost to replace the property, with materials of like kind and quality, less an amount determined for physical depreciation. This valuation clause does not correspond to book value because book value is based upon the original purchase price rather than the "cost to replace the property." For this reason, book value should not be used for insurance purposes because substantial underinsurance could result.

Coverage can also be purchased on a *replacement cost* basis in lieu of the ACV valuation. When replacement cost coverage is indicated on the policy's declaration page, the organization will be reimbursed for the cost to replace the property with no deduction for physical depreciation. Replacement cost coverage can be effected for little or no charge; however, the insurable value for the property will be greater and therefore the policy's premium will be somewhat greater. Even when replacement cost coverage is purchased, the policy will only pay actual cash value if the property is not repaired or replaced. Therefore, organizations that would replace a building or premises following its destruction by fire or other peril should insure it on a replacement cost basis. On the other hand, if the building would not be replaced, actual cash value insurance should be purchased.

9. Buy "All Risk" Property Insurance

For property insurance coverage on buildings, contents, inventory, etc., there are several standard policy forms that may be purchased to insure against different perils.

Named Perils Coverage. The *basic form* provides coverage for direct loss caused by the specifically listed perils of fire, lightning, explosion, windstorm, hail, smoke, aircraft, vehicles, riot, civil commotion, vandalism, sprinkler leakage, sink hole collapse, and volcanic action. The *broad form* expands the perils covered to also include glass breakage, falling objects, weight of ice, sleet, or snow, water damage, and limited collapse coverage. The third option, the *special form*, covers all risks of physical loss unless the loss-causing peril is specifically excluded from coverage.

All Risk Coverage. The special form property policy provides broader coverage than either the basic or broad form policies. In essence, this form provides what has historically been called *all risk* property insurance coverage. Typically, all risk insurance does provide broader insurance protection than does *named peril* insurance such as that provided by the basic and broad form policies. In addition, all risk insurance places a higher burden of proof on the insurer in order to deny a claim than does named perils insurance. Under an all risk policy, an insurer must demonstrate that a loss falls within the policy's exclusions in order to deny a claim. With a named peril policy, on the other hand, it is up to the insured to prove that a loss falls within the insured perils of the policy. For these reasons, all risk coverage is generally preferred over named perils coverage.

10. Don't Overlook "Time Element" Exposures

Property insurance policies cover only direct loss to insured property caused by insured perils. However, damage to insured property may also lead to a type of indirect loss, usually referred to as a *time element* loss—one that results from a covered peril but is not caused directly by it. Time element losses include such losses as business interruption, extra expense, rental value, and leasehold interest. Obtaining proper coverage for indirect losses is very important since, in many cases, these losses can far exceed the direct physical loss to property.

Business Interruption Insurance. The most common of the indirect loss coverages is called *business interruption* or *business income* insurance. This coverage is designed to reimburse the insured who suffers a direct property loss for any loss of earnings that results during the period required to restore the property to its normal operating condition. For example, a manufacturer would suffer a severe loss of sales after a major fire at its warehouse destroyed inventory that would have been sold. In order for business interruption insurance to reimburse the insured for loss of earnings, the physical damage must be caused by a covered peril. If this is the case and an interruption of business occurs, the insurance company will pay for both lost net profit and expenses that continue even though operations have ceased (e.g., salaries of executive officers, insurance premiums, lease or rental expenses, taxes, etc.). Coverage is limited to the length of time required, with the exercise of due diligence, to repair, rebuild, or replace the part of the property that has been damaged or destroyed.

Extra Expense Insurance.   Some types of organizations have no need for business interruption insurance because their operations can or must be continued even though their premises are damaged or destroyed. For example, hospitals, banks, and newspapers would generally desire to continue operations at all costs in order to avoid losing customers and to fulfill what they perceive as their moral commitments to their customers and communities. To help pay for the extra costs associated with continuing operations at a temporary location, *extra expense insurance* is available. Extra expense insurance covers the necessary extra expenses required in order to continue normal operations following damage or loss by covered peril to insured property. It will, for example, reimburse the insured for the costs associated with paying overtime to employees, advertising the new location, renting necessary equipment, renting a facility, and so forth.

Leasehold Interest and Rental Income.   If an organization is leasing property (e.g., office space) in a long-term contract, it is possible that the current lease agreement calls for a rental payment which is significantly less than the cost of renting comparable property in the current market. Since many leases call for the termination of the lease in the event the property becomes untenantable because of a fire or other peril, the occurrence of such a peril and the subsequent cancellation of the lease could cause an indirect loss to the organization equivalent to the additional cost of renting comparable space. *Leasehold interest* insurance is available to insure against the additional cost of renting comparable space under these circumstances.

Likewise, if the organization leases space to others, a loss of rental income would occur if the property were damaged to the point that lease provisions call for termination of the lease. *Rental value* insurance is available to reimburse the organization for this type of income loss.

Appendix C

Evaluating Insurer Solvency

The business manager should always remember that the least costly insurance is no bargain if the insurer is unable, or unwilling, to respond to a loss when one does occur. Unfortunately, an insurer's ability to pay its claims is often overlooked. When considering placing your business with a particular insurer, it is important to carefully evaluate the current financial position of that insurer in order to avoid unpaid claims, potential interruption of coverage, inability to recover unearned premiums, and the inconvenience of state guaranty funds. This appendix reviews several approaches the business manager may use to examine an insurer's financial integrity.

State Guaranty Associations

While state guaranty or security associations have been established as mechanisms for reimbursing policyholders and third-party claimants of insolvent admitted insurers, relying solely on these guaranty funds for protection against insurer insolvency is not recommended for several reasons:

- Reimbursement amounts payable by the guaranty fund are generally subject to a deductible and a maximum limit of liability (e.g., $50,000).
- Many guaranty funds make no allowance for the return of unearned premiums.
- Long delays in payments are frequent, due mainly to litigation between

the state regulators and the owner/managers of the insolvent company.

- Guaranty funds are not applicable to nonadmitted insurers, surplus lines carriers, life and health insurers, and fidelity insurers (though separate insolvency funds may exist in some states for some of these carriers).

- Guaranty funds are not designed to accommodate the insolvency of a major insurance company or multiple insolvencies among medium-sized insurance companies.

In short, while state guaranty funds may provide some protection, it is a mistake to rely solely upon them without making some effort to choose fiscally responsible insurance companies.

Evaluating Insurers

Fortunately, there are several sources of information which can help business managers and their agents/brokers to identify insurers with financial difficulties. These sources include publications of the A. M. Best Company, Standard & Poors Corporate Rating, and certain subjective information.

Best's Insurance Reports

Since 1900, the A. M. Best Company has provided a rating service which assigns insurers alphabetical ratings based upon their overall financial performance. These alphabetical ratings are further clarified by modifiers. In addition, the financial size of insurers is indicated by Roman numerals and is based on policyholder's surplus. The results of Best's analyses are published annually in *Best's Insurance Reports*. Rating and financial size categories are broken down as indicated in Figure C.1.

Figure C.1. Best rating sytem.

Best rating	*Rating modifiers*
A+ – Superior	"c" – Contingent rating
A – Excellent	"w" – Watch list
B+ – Very good	"x" – Revised rating
B – Good	"s" – Consolidated rating
C+ – Fairly good	"e" – Parent rating
C – Fair	"r" – Reinsured rating
	"p" – Pooled rating
	"g" – Group rating

"Not assigned" classification

NA-2 – Less than minimum size

NA-3 – Insufficient experience

NS-4 – Rating procedure inapplicable

NA-5 – Significant change

NA-6 – Reinsured by unrated reinsurer

NA-7 – Below minimum standards

NA-8 – Incomplete financial information

NA-9 – Company request

NA-10 – Under state supervision

Financial size rating

Financial size category	*Adjusted policyholders' surplus (in millions of dollars)*
Class I	Up to $1.0
Class II	.1 to 2
Class III	.2 to 5
Class IV	.5 to 10
Class V	.10 to 25
Class VI	.25 to 50
Class VII	.50 to 100
Class VIII	.100 to 150
Class IX	.250 to 500
Class X	.500 to 750
Class XI	.750 to 1.000
Class XII	.1,000 to 1,250
Class XIII	.1,250 to 1,500
Class XIV	.1,500 to 2,000
Class XV	.2,000 or more

Figure C.1. Best rating system.

While it is generally recommended that insurance be purchased from a company rated A+ or A, this is not always possible. For example, the principal market for a specialty line of coverage (e.g., professional liability) may have a lower rating. When this is the case, other factors, such as financial size and reputation, should be considered. While knowledge of an insurer's current Best's rating is helpful, the historical trend of its ratings over the past 3 to 5 years is usually more revealing. As a general rule, if two companies have the same rating, it is considered safer to pick the company which has improved its Best's rating in recent years rather than one whose rating has declined. For example, a B+ insurer whose rating was recently raised from a B is probably more stable than a B+ insurer whose rating was recently lowered from an A and who held an A+ rating 2 years before.

Standard & Poors Corporate Ratings

Standard & Poors, primarily known for its debt-rating services, offers an insurer rating service based on an insurer's claims-paying ability. Standard & Poors ratings reflect a current assessment of the insurer's financial ability to meet its obligation under its insurance contracts while recognizing the financial capabilities of its reinsurers. Ratings are determined by a review of statutory financial statements and information from top company management. Standard & Poors defines its ratings as follows:

AAA	Extremely strong ability to meet contractual policy obligations
AA	Very strong ability to meet contractual policy obligations
A	Strong ability to meet contractual policy obligations
BBB	Adequate ability to meet contractual policy obligations
BB, B, or C	Uncertain or weak capacity to meet contractual policy obligations, with CCC assigned to companies with the weakest or most uncertain capacity
D	Insolvent and~or in receivership

These ratings are published in the Standard & Poors publication *Credit Week* or can otherwise be obtained by telephoning the S & P rating desk in New York City. The number is (212) 248-2551. The drawback to this system is that Standard & Poors rates an insurer only upon the request of that insurer, who initiates the rating process and must therefore pay for the service. The insurer also retains the privilege of refusing to have the rating published if dissatisfied with the results. For this reason, low ratings are not likely ever to become public knowledge. However, an insurance company that is rated by Standard & Poors is likely to be in a strong financial position.

Other Evaluation Criteria

State insurance regulators have developed a series of financial ratios designed to indicate the financial strengths and weaknesses of insurance companies. These ratios, formerly known as the Early Warning System, have been renamed the Insurance Regulatory Information System (IRIS). IRIS consists of 11 financial ratios that are provided to insurance regulators for their solvency reviews. These ratios are developed by periodically examining the financial statements of insurers that have been judged insolvent and selecting key indicators so that the repetition of past mistakes can be prevented. Unfortunately, computed results of these ratios are not made available to the public by the National Association of Insurance Commissioners. However, the A. M. Best Company does make its own computations of these ratios and reports them in *Best's Trend Report*, which is published every June. As with Best's ratings, it is important to look at trends in IRIS ratios rather than only at the current year's results.

In addition to Best's ratings, Standard & Poors ratings, and IRIS tests, there are also other indicators of a more subjective nature that may help business managers and agents/brokers identify companies with potential financial problems. A few signs of potential financial problems include:

- A marketing strategy more aggressive than that of the general marketplace may indicate a pressing need for cash.
- Carriers who are routinely slow in paying claims and frequently question legitimate losses may be having cash flow problems.
- Fluctuations in management philosophy, high turnover in management personnel, and a lack of cooperation from management in responding to inquiries into financial matters may indicate financial distress.
- Refusal of premium finance companies or banks to finance premiums for a particular carrier may indicate that they are concerned about the insured's financial position.
- Abrupt severance of an insurance company's relationship with its accountants and/or legal advisors may indicate disputes over the need to disclose unfavorable financial information.
- High claims complaint ratios (which are available from many states' insurance departments) may indicate a desire to conserve cash by intentionally paying claims slowly, cutting staff, denying legitimate claims, or delaying the refund of unearned premiums.

Effective sources of such evaluation criteria include professional associations and networks of agents, brokers, and policyholders as well as insurance trade journals, publications, state insurance departments, and the financial reports of the insurer. This is an area in which the business manager must place a great amount of reliance upon the agent/broker, and it is suggested that the agent or broker be questioned as to steps taken by the firm to monitor the financial ability of the insurers it represents.

Summary

The insolvency of an insurance company can cause many problems for a business manager and agent/broker alike. Furthermore, state guaranty funds are not an answer to these problems. The long-term financial stability of an insurer should be carefully evaluated by assessing the sources of information mentioned in this appendix before placing business with that insurer. A little research before the policy is first written can prevent a great deal of future trouble. In addition, it will often be prudent to pay higher premiums to a financially strong insurance company than to spend less money buying insurance from an insurer that may not be around to pay claims under the policies it issues.

Glossary

101 Insurance Acronyms and Abbreviations

ACV	Actual cash value
AL	Automobile liability
AOP	All other perils
BI	Bodily injury, business interruption
BPF	Basic premium factor
CCC	Care, custody, or control (exclusion)
CEBS	Certified Employee Benefits Specialist
CERCLA	Comprehensive Environmental Response Compensation and Liability Act
ChFC	Chartered Financial Consultant
CGL	Commercial general liability
CIC	Certified Insurance Counselor
CIF	Cost, insurance, and freight
CLU	Chartered Life Underwriter
C/O	Completed operations
CPCU	Chartered Property Casualty Underwriter
CSP	Certified Safety Professional
DIC	Difference in conditions (insurance)
EAP	Employee assistance program
EEOC	Equal Employment Opportunity Commission
EIL	Environmental impairment liability
EL	Employers liability
ELP	Excess loss premium (factor)
E & O	Errors and omissions (liability)
ERISA	Employee Retirement Income Security Act
ERP	Extended reporting period

E & S	Excess and surplus (lines)
FAS	Free along side
FCAS	Fellow of the Casualty Actuarial Society
FCIA	Foreign Credit Insurance Association
FCIC	Federal Crop Insurance Corporation
FC&S	Free of capture and seizure
FM	Factory Mutual
FOB	Free on board
FR	Fire resistive
FSA	Fellow of the Society of Actuaries
FTCAC	Fire, theft, and combined additional coverage
GL	Garage liability, general liability
HO	Homeowners (insurance)
HPL	Hospital professional liability
HPR	Highly protected risk
IBNR	Incurred but not reported
IDBI	Industrial development bond insurance
IGF	Insurance guaranteed financing
IH	Industrial hygiene
IIAA	Independent Insurance Agents of America
IRIS	Insurance Regulatory Information System
IRMI	International Risk Management Institute, Inc.
IRPM	Individual risk premium modification
ISO	Insurance Services Office
JSA	Job safety analysis
K&R	Kidnap and ransom
LCF	Loss conversion factor
LOC	Letter of credit
MGA	Managing general agency
MIB	Medical Information Bureau
MOP	Manufacturers output policy
MORT	Management oversight and risk tree
MP	Minimum premium
MTC	Motor truck cargo (insurance)
MVR	Motor vehicle record
NAIB	National Association of Insurance Brokers
NAIC	National Association of Insurance Commissioners

NCCI	National Council on Compensation Insurance
NIOSH	National Institute for Occupational Safety and Health
NOC	Not otherwise classified
NP	Named perils
NPD	No payroll division
NPV	Net present value
OASDHI	Old age, survivorship, disability, and health insurance
OCIP	Owner-controlled insurance program
OCP	Owners and contractors protective (liability insurance)
OCSLA	Outer Continental Shelf Lands Act
OD	Occupational disease
OEE	Operators extra expense (insurance)
OL&T	Owners, landlords, and tenants (liability insurance)
OPIC	Overseas Private Investment Corporation
OSHA	Occupational Safety and Health Act
PD	Property damage
PI	Personal injury
P&I	Protection and indemnity (insurance)
PIA	Professional Insurance Agents (association)
PIP	Personal injury protection
PL	Professional liability
PMI	Private mortgage insurance
PRIMA	Public Risk and Insurance Management Association
RC	Replacement cost
RFP	Request for proposal
RIMS	Risk and Insurance Management Society
RMIS	Risk management information system
SIR	Self-insured retention
SMP	Special multi-peril (package policy)
TM	Tax multiplier
UCR	Usual, customary, reasonable (reimbursement)
UL	Underwriter's Laboratories, umbrella liability
UM	Uninsured motorist
U&O	Use and occupancy
USL&H	United States Longshore and Harbor Workers' (Compensation Act)
V&MM	Vandalism and malicious mischief

VSI   Vendors single interest (insurance)

WC   Workers compensation

XCU   Explosion, collapse, and underground (property damage hazard)

101 Insurance Definitions

Accounts receivable coverage: insures against loss to accounts receivable which may be uncollectible through damage to records caused by an insured peril. Included in this coverage is interest on loans to offset collections and additional expenses resulting from impaired records. This coverage may be written on a monthly reporting basis for large organizations or on a nonreporting form for smaller firms.

Actual cash value (ACV): a term used in property insurance to denote the measure of recovery at the time of loss. ACV equals the cost to replace the damaged property less depreciation of that damaged property. The depreciation used is not the same as that used for accounting purposes but is an estimate of actual physical depreciation. "Book value" should never be used to establish insurable values because depreciation schedules used for accounting purposes do not correlate with physical depreciation.

Actuary: an individual, often holding a professional designation, who computes statistics relating to insurance. Actuaries are most frequently used to estimate loss reserves and develop premiums. Professional designations are awarded by the Casualty Actuarial Society and the Society of Actuaries.

Admitted company: a company licensed to do business in a specified jurisdiction. For example, a company licensed to do business in Georgia is an admitted company in that state.

Advisory rates: judgment rates, called "(a) rates," which do not have loss experience statistics as a foundation for their development. These rates are developed by the rating bureaus and modified by underwriters on an individual risk basis according to what they feel is an equitable rate commensurate with the risk involved.

Aggregate: the maximum amount payable by an insurance carrier on behalf of a policyholder during any given annual policy period. Aggregate limits may be equal to or greater than the per occurrence or per accident policy limit. An insurance policy may have one or more aggregate limits. For example, the standard commercial general liability policy has two: the general aggregate that applies to all claims except those that fall in the products-completed operations hazard and a separate products-completed operations aggregate.

Agreed amount clause: a provision in fire insurance policies covering certain classes of property, whereby the coinsurance clause is suspended if the insured carries an amount of insurance specified by the company (usually 90 percent or more of value).

All risk insurance: protection from loss arising out of any fortuitous cause other than those perils or causes specifically excluded by name. This is in contrast to other policies which name the peril or perils insured against. All risk insurance is usually preferred over named perils insurance because it usually provides broader coverage and because it places a greater burden of proof on an insurer wishing to deny a claim.

Annual aggregate deductible: a situation that occurs when a policyholder agrees to assume the payment of claims incurred up to a stated aggregate amount. Once the policyholder makes claims payments up to the agreed amount during a policy year, any additional claims are paid to the insured by the "excess aggregate" insurer on a monthly or quarterly basis as reported.

Associate in Risk Management (ARM): a designation conferred upon individuals who successfully complete three written comprehensive examinations administered by the Insurance Institute of America. The three exams are: essentials of risk management, essentials of risk control, and risk financing.

Bailee's customers insurance: an inland marine policy that protects the insured from claims by its customers for damage to or destruction of customer property in the insured's care, custody, or control. This policy is needed by such firms as dry cleaners, jewelers, repairers, and furriers.

Basic extended reporting period: 60-day and 5-year extended reporting periods of the ISO commercial general liability policy that are known, collectively, as the basic extended reporting period (BERP). The BERP is automatically provided to the insured by the 1986 ISO claims-made CGL policy when the policy is canceled, not renewed, renewed with a laser exclusion, renewed on a basis other than claims-made, or renewed with an advanced retroactive date. See also: Extended Reporting Period and Supplemental Extended Reporting Period.

Basic limits: the minimum limits of liability of auto insurance or commercial general liability insurance which can be purchased by a policyholder. The *manual rates* are for basic limits, and *increase limits factors* are used to increase the rates for higher limits of liability.

Basic premium factor: a factor used in the retrospective formula to represent expenses of the insurance carrier, such as for acquisition, audit, administration, and profit or contingencies other than taxes.

Basket retention: used in connection with self-insurance. This excess liability insurance is triggered (attaches) when retained losses for several lines of coverage (e.g., workers compensation and general liability) reach a certain specified level.

Binder: a legal agreement issued by either an agent or a company to provide temporary insurance until a policy can be written. It should contain a definite time limit, should be in writing, and should clearly designate the company in which the risk is bound as well as the amount, the perils insured against, and the type of insurance.

Blanket coverage: policy coverage applying a single limit to any number of scheduled or nonscheduled locations.

Blanket position bond: insures an employer against loss from dishonest acts by employees. This type of bond is a multi-penalty contract, and its amount of liability applies separately to each employee identified as the defaulter.

Bodily injury liability coverage: protection against loss arising out of the liability imposed upon the insured by law for damages due to bodily injury, sickness, or disease sustained by any person or persons (other than employees). This is one of the types of coverages (property damage liability being the other) provided by general and auto liability insurance.

Boiler and machinery insurance: insurance against loss arising from the operation of boilers and machinery. It may cover loss suffered by the boilers or the machinery itself, or it may include damage done to other property and business interruption (use and occupancy) losses.

Builders risk: indemnifies for loss of or damage to a building under construction. Insurance is normally written for a specified amount on the building and applies only in the course of construction. Coverage is usually on an all risk basis. The builders risk policy also may include coverage for items in transit to the construction site (up to a certain percentage of value) as well as items stored at the site.

Business auto policy: a standard automobile policy that can be used to insure physical damage to owned or hired autos and liability arising from owned, hired, or nonowned commercial automobiles. The BAP's physical damage coverage can include *collision, comprehensive,* and/or *named perils* coverage. Uninsured motorists coverage and medical payments coverage may be added by endorsement.

Business income insurance: protection against loss of earnings of a business during the time required to rebuild or repair property damaged or destroyed by fire or some other insured peril. The coverage is also called *use and occupancy* or *business interruption.* Business interruption losses are often greater than the direct damage losses that cause the interruption, and careful consideration should be given to insuring this exposure. Business managers should also determine if they have and should insure a *contingent business interruption* exposure. This type of exposure arises when the business is dependent on a key supplier or key customer that could experience a fire or major catastrophe that would make it unable to continue supplying component parts or purchasing the insured business' products.

Captive insurer: merely a do-it-yourself insurance company. A captive insurer or insurance subsidiary normally insures the risks and exposures of its parent company and affiliates, or it may be owned by a number of companies in the same industry insuring risks common to the group. Usually, but not always, captives operate as reinsurers rather than direct insurers. An admitted insurance company (called a fronting company) issues the policies and then reinsures them with the captive. This approach allows the captive to avoid the expense and trouble of becoming licensed in all 50 states.

Captives can be further identified by type: namely, pure captives (those that write no outside business), association captives, senior captives (captives that have a long operating history), and profit center captives (captives begun with profit potential in mind).

Care, custody, and control (CCC): a standard property damage liability exclusion found in most liability insurance policies. This exclusion precludes coverage for property which is in the care, custody, or control of the insured.

The exclusion may be worded so that it applies either to personal property only or to all property. Some companies will occasionally consider removing or modifying the exclusion on a specific or blanket basis.

Cargo insurance: marine insurance covering cargo being transported by a commercial carrier or other carrier.

Cargo legal liability: insurance purchased by firms transporting the property of others which covers their legal liability for damage to that property.

Certificate of insurance: a document which evidences that an insurance policy has been issued and shows the amount and type of insurance provided. Certificates of insurance are often required by lenders to show that financed property is insured. Contractors and subcontractors providing services to the business manager should also be required to provide insurance certificates. It is important to note that an insurance certificate is not a contract and does not place any obligations on the insurance company. Certificates are only a statement that insurance policies are in effect on the date they are issued.

Chartered Property Casualty Underwriter (CPCU): a professional designation within the insurance industry identifying an individual who has satisfactorily completed 10 college-level examinations and met ethical and experience requirements. The 10 examinations cover the following topics: commercial liability insurance, commercial property insurance, personal lines insurance, risk management, insurance issues and professional ethics, insurance company operations, insurance law, management, accounting and finance, and economics.

Claims-made: a liability policy that will cover claims made (reported or filed) during the year the policy is in force for any incidents which occur that year or during any previous period the policyholder was insured under the *claims-made* contract. This form of coverage is in contrast to the occurrence policy, which covers today's incident regardless of whether a claim is filed 1 or more years later.

Claims-made multiplier: a factor applied to rates used for a *claims-made* commercial general liability policy, depending upon how long an insured has been in a claims-made program. It reduces the premium in the early years of a claims-made program to recognize the insured's reduced exposure because of the retroactive date. The insured receives a larger credit in the initial year of the claims-made program, and the credit is reduced in each subsequent year (unless the retro date is advanced). The credit virtually disappears in the 5th claims-made year.

Coinsurance: a policy provision requiring the insured to carry insurance equal to a specified percentage of the value of the property covered. It provides for the full payment, up to the amount of the policy, of all losses if the insured has insurance at least equal to the specified percentage of the value of the property covered, or if the loss is equal to or exceeds the coinsurance percentage of the value of the property covered. The loss payment, in the case of most partial losses, is reduced proportionately if the amount of insurance falls short of the named percentage. The formula: amount of insurance purchased divided by the amount required multiplied by the loss equals the amount paid.

In health insurance and some other specialized property and liability insurance, the coinsurance clause requires the insured to pay a percentage of any loss. In these situations, the clause is used to discourage malingering in the hospital or, in the case of property and liability policies, to encourage loss control.

Commercial general liability (CGL) policy: a broad form of liability insurance which covers business organizations against liability claims for bodily injury and property damage arising out of their operations, products and completed operations, and independent contractors (but excluding coverage for liability arising out of the use of automobiles). Contractual liability and personal injury/advertising liability coverages are also usually covered by the CGL. Contractual liability coverage insures the liability of others for which the insured agrees to be responsible in a business contract or lease. Personal injury/advertising injury liability coverage insures against false arrest and libel, slander, defamation of character, and disparagement of goods communicated by the insured's employees or in its advertising activities.

Contractual liability: liability that is passed from one party to another in a *hold harmless* or *indemnity* agreement. For example, a tenant in a building may hold the landlord harmless for any bodily injury sustained by the public in the premises. If an injured party sues the landlord, the tenant will have to hire an attorney to defend the landlord and pay any judgments made against the landlord. Contractual liability insurance covers this exposure.

Cross liability: a situation that can arise when more than one organization is insured by a liability policy, e.g., commercial general liability (CGL) insurance. In that situation, one insured may injure or damage the property of and become legally liable to another insured. It may therefore be important for the insurance policy to cover the *cross liability* of one insured to another. Most CGL and umbrella liability policies contain a *severability of interest* clause that allows coverage for cross liability suits by stipulating that the policy covers each insured as if each were insured by a separate policy (except with respect to the policy limits).

Dividends: the return of premium to an insured by the insurance company. Policies on which dividends may be paid are often called *participating insurance*. Dividends are most commonly used with workers compensation insurance, but general and automobile policies can also be participating policies. General liability and auto policy dividend programs are particularly common in Louisiana and Texas. There are different types of dividend programs. A *flat dividend* involves the payment of a flat percentage of the premium. A *sliding scale dividend* program bases the percentage to be paid on the insured's loss experience; the lower the losses, the higher the dividend. A *retention plan* is essentially the same as a sliding scale dividend plan, but the mechanics are slightly different.

It is important to note that it is illegal for insurers to guarantee that dividends will be paid. Consider the possibility that the dividend will be reduced or omitted entirely when evaluating dividend plans. Research into the insurer's dividend-payment history can facilitate this analysis.

Employers liability coverage: a coverage that comes into play when, for one reason or another, an injured employee's claim is not covered under workers compensation law. In such a case, the employee usually files a lawsuit against the employer. This type of suit is not covered by the workers compensation coverage of the policy (which applies only to benefits required under workers compensation law). It is also excluded by the commercial general liability policy. To avoid a potential gap, employers liability coverage is included in the workers compensation policy. It pays on behalf of the insured (employer) all sums which the insured becomes legally obligated to pay as damages because of bodily injury by accident or disease sustained by any employee arising out of and in the course of his or her employment.

Experience modifier: factor developed by measuring the difference between the insured's actual past loss experience and the expected loss experience of that type of business. This factor may be either a debit or a credit. A debit increases the premium, while a credit decreases it. When applied to the manual premium, the experience modification produces a premium that is more representative of an insured's actual past loss experience.

Exposure basis: basis to which rates are applied to determine premium. Exposures may be measured by payroll (as in workers compensation), receipts, sales, square footage, area, or worker-hours (as in general liability), per unit (as in automobile insurance), or per $1,000 of value (as in property insurance). The exposure base for a particular insured is multiplied by the manual rate to determine the manual premium.

Extended reporting period (ERP): a designated period of time after a claims-made policy has expired during which a claim may be made and coverage triggered as if the claim had been made during the policy period. An ERP covers only claims that stem from accidents or events that took place prior to the policy's expiration date and after its retroactive date, if there is one. See also: Basic Extended Reporting Period and Supplemental Extended Reporting Period.

Extra expense insurance: coverage for businesses that would probably not shut down in the event of major physical damage to the property and would find it imperative to remain in operation. If a business is such that it could lose most of its customers during the temporary curtailment of its services, or if its services are vital to the public, then it needs extra expense coverage to insure against the extra cost of keeping the business operating despite damage to or destruction of existing facilities. Common examples of businesses that purchase extra expense insurance are newspapers, hospitals, banks, oil and gas distributors, and public utilities. Coverage can be combined with business interruption insurance.

Flat cancellation: the cancellation of a policy as of its effective date, before the company has assumed liability. This requires the full return of paid premiums.

Fronting company: an insurance company which issues an insurance policy to the insured and then reinsures all or most of the risk with the insured's captive insurance company or elsewhere as directed by the insured. The fronting company may or may not provide claims adjusting or other services. A percentage of the premium is retained by the fronting company as a fee. This approach allows the insured to issue certificates of insurance acceptable to regulators and lenders and avoids the burden of licensing the insured's captive in all states or of becoming a qualified self-insurer.

Garagekeepers liability: provides coverage to owners of parking garages, parking lots, body and repair shops, and similar businesses for liability as bailees with respect to damage to automobiles left in their custody for safekeeping or repair. Coverage is contingent upon establishing liability on the part of the insured.

Guaranteed cost insurance: premium charged on a prospective basis but not on the basis of loss experience during the policy period. While an experience modifier derived from loss experience in past years may be used, there are no adjustments made to recognize the current year's loss experience. The only adjustment to the premium made after the policy year is to recognize the insured's actual exposure during the year. In other words, the premium is estimated at the beginning of the policy period based on estimated payroll, receipts, or whatever exposure base applies. At the end of the year, the actual payroll or other exposure base is determined, usually by a premium auditor, and is multiplied by the appropriate rate to yield the actual premium.

Highly protected risk (HPR): a term referring to industrial and commercial risks which meet high property protection standards. Risks of this kind are almost always protected by sprinklers. The Factory Mutual Insurers and Industrial Risk Insurers will only insure highly protected risks.

Incurred but not reported (IBNR): recognition that events have taken place in such a manner as to eventually produce claims but that these events have not yet been reported. In other words, IBNR is a loss that has happened but is not known about. Since it is impossible to know the value of a case not yet reported or investigated, a subjective estimate is often used by insurance companies to recognize losses incurred but not reported.

Incurred losses: generally means all open and closed claims occurring within a fixed period, usually a year. Incurred losses customarily are computed in accordance with the following formula: losses paid during the period plus an estimate of the value of outstanding claims at the end of the period minus outstanding losses at the beginning of the period. Incurred losses include reserves for open claims.

Inland marine: insurance originally developed by marine underwriters to cover goods while in transit by other than ocean vessels. It now includes any goods in transit, except transocean, as well as insurance for certain types of personal property, with the essential condition being that the insured property be movable. For example, floater policies covering equipment, tools, musical instruments, cameras, or jewelry are considered inland marine policies. Bridges and tunnels are also considered as inland marine because they act as instruments of transportation.

Insurance department: a regulatory department charged with the administration of insurance laws and other responsibilities associated with insurance. Insurance regulators determine or approve acceptable rates and policy forms for many lines of insurance and monitor the financial position of insurers operating in their states. They may also help members of the public who have disputes with an insurer. The commissioner of insurance is the head of this department in most states.

Insurance Services Office (ISO): a nonprofit insurer association that collects statistical information, promulgates and files insurance rates with regulators, and drafts standard insurance policy forms for most lines of insurance (except workers compensation and surety). Insurance Services Office is supported on an assessment basis by its member insurance companies.

Laser exclusion: an exclusionary endorsement under a claims-made policy which excludes liability arising from the products, locations, accidents, or work specified in the endorsement.

Lloyd's of London: one of the oldest professional risk bearers in the world, Lloyd's of London is not an insurance company. Instead, groups of individuals join "syndicates" which assume liability through an underwriter. Each individual independently and personally assumes a proportionate part of the insurance accepted by the underwriter. While Lloyd's is best known for the unusual policies it often writes for entertainers, it is a very significant part of the world reinsurance community.

Longshore and Harbor Workers' Compensation Act (LHWCA): a federal act requiring employers to compensate injured longshoremen and harbor workers. LHWCA benefits are higher than those of most states, which makes insurance coverage under the act more expensive than for state compensation acts. This exposure may be insured commercially, or the employer can file to become a qualified self-insurer. The classifications of persons falling under the provisions of this act are broadening with time.

Loss constant: a flat amount added to the premium of a workers compensation policy that is lower than the minimum amount for experience rating. It is designed to offset the worse-than-average loss experience often encountered on smaller risks.

Loss limitation for retrospective rating and retention plans: a limitation possible under retrospective rating plans: the losses used in computing the premium are limited to a selected amount. The effects of *shock losses* that would otherwise fall into the calculations of final retrospective or retention plan premium are thereby reduced. There is an additional premium charged for the loss limitation.

Loss reserve: an estimate of the value of a claim or group of claims not yet paid. A case reserve is an estimate of the amount for which a particular claim will ultimately be settled or adjudicated. Insurers will also set reserves for their entire books of business to estimate their future liabilities.

Loss trending: predicting future losses through an analysis of past losses. Past loss data must span a sufficient number of years (5 or more) with a preference for the most recent years, since they most closely approximate current exposure. Loss history must be considered in the light of exposure data, any anticipated changes in company operations or structure, inflation, workers compensation benefit changes, and any other input relevant to projection of future losses.

Manual rates: full rates as promulgated by Insurance Services Office (general liability, automobile) and the National Council on Compensation Insurance (workers compensation) before application of any credits or deviations. The rates are determined by looking them up in a rating manual, hence their name. By law these rates are supposed to be adequate, reasonable, and nondiscriminatory.

Mature claims-made policy: a claims-made CGL policy in at least its 5th consecutive year. When claims-made insurance is first written for a business, premiums are discounted to recognize the reduced possibility that the policy will be triggered because of the retroactive date provision. The amount of the discount decreases each year until it is eliminated in the 5th year. A claims-made CGL policy that is in at least its 5th consecutive claims-made year without advancement of the retroactive date is "mature." No premium discounts (claims-made multipliers) are applied in rating mature claims-made policies.

Midi-tail: a term used for an extended reporting period longer than 60 days but not of unlimited duration. The 1986 ISO claims-made commercial general liability (CGL) policy midi-tail is for 5 years. The CGL's midi-tail applies only for known and reported circumstances in most cases.

Minimum premium: the lowest premium that may be charged for an insurance policy. The minimum premium is charged for a policy when the manual premium (manual rates times exposure basis) is lower than the minimum premium. Sometimes policies, particularly umbrellas written in the excess and surplus lines marketplace, are subject to a quoted "minimum and deposit premium." This is the minimum premium to be charged for the coverage, and even cancellation of the policy by the insured will not result in a return of the premium.

Mobile equipment: equipment such as earth movers, tractors, diggers, farm machinery, and forklifts that, even though self-propelled, is not considered an automobile for insurance purposes. Liability arising from mobile equipment is covered by the commercial general liability policy. Normally, it should not be insured in the auto policy. Physical damage coverage is usually provided by an "equipment floater."

Monopolistic state funds: compulsory funds in jurisdictions where employers must obtain workers compensation insurance from the state. Such insurance is not subject to any of the procedures or programs of the National Council on Compensation Insurance. Insurance companies may not write workers compensation insurance in the monopolistic fund states: Nevada, North Dakota, Ohio, Puerto Rico, Washington, West Virginia, and Wyoming.

Mortgage (mortgagee) clause: a fire insurance policy provision covering mortgaged property. It specifies that the mortgagee has interest in the property and that first right of recovery shall not be defeated by any act of neglect of the insured. Loan documents usually require that the lender be included as mortgagee on the property insurance.

Mutual insurance company: an insurer owned and operated by and for its policyholders. Every owner of the company is a policyholder; every policyholder is an owner. Any profits made are usually returned to policyholders as dividends.

Named perils: perils that are insured against by specific mention in *named peril* policies. These are distinguished from *all risk* policies, which insure against all perils except those that are specifically excluded. Named perils often include: fire, lightning, smoke, vandalism, malicious mischief, windstorm, hail, explosion, collision, and collapse. Some optional perils that may or may not be insured include: flood, earthquake, volcanic eruption, sinkhole collapse, and damage from molten material.

National Council on Workers Compensation Insurance (NCCI): a voluntary nonprofit unincorporated association formed in 1915. Its duties are the promulgation and administration of workers compensation insurance rates and policy forms. Its membership is comprised of stock and mutual insurers, reciprocals, and state funds. The National Council is a filing agency and rating organization in 31 jurisdictions, and it serves as an advisory or service organization in many states where independent or state bureaus exist.

Occupational disease: an impairment of health caused by exposure to conditions arising out of or in the course of one's employment. This is distinguishable from impairment of health caused by accident. State workers compensation laws vary as to the compensability of occupational disease.

Occurrence insurance: coverage for an *occurrence*, usually defined in liability policies as an accident, including continuous or repeated exposure to conditions, which results in bodily injury or property damage neither expected nor intended from the standpoint of the insured. Occurrence policies cover injury or damage that occurs during the policy period irrespective of when the claim is made against the insured. This is in contrast to a claims-made policy that covers only claims made during the policy period.

Paid loss retrospective rating: an insurance cash flow plan that allows the insured to hold loss reserves until they are paid out in claims. It is used most frequently with workers compensation and other liability lines. It utilizes the standard and retrospective rating formulas, but only paid claims, rather than incurred (paid and reserved) claims, are plugged into the formula. Because the insurer has a substantial credit risk, these plans are usually collateralized with a letter of credit.

Payout profile: schedule illustrating the percentage of loss dollars actually paid in settlement of claims over time. On the average, less than $.28 of the total loss dollar for workers compensation claims is paid during the 1st year of coverage. Even less is paid on the average for general liability claims. It may be 7 to 10 years later before $.99 of the loss dollar is paid. Therefore, unpaid loss reserves can generate significant investment income to the holder.

Premium audit: a review of the records of the insured company by an insurance company representative, the premium auditor, to determine the actual exposure base and premium due on a policy such as workers compensation. At policy inception, the premium is based on an estimate of the exposure base. The purpose of the premium audit is to determine what the exposure actually was during the insured period. The actual exposure is then applied to the previously agreed upon rates to determine the final premium.

Peril: the cause of a loss (e.g., fire, windstorm, explosion, hail, riot, vandalism, strike, malicious mischief, earthquake, flood, sinkhole collapse, volcanic eruption, etc.).

Pool: an organization of insurers or reinsurers through which particular types of risks are underwritten with premiums, losses, and expenses shared in agreed ratios.

A group of organizations not large enough to self-insure individually can form a shared risk pool.

Premium discount: a volume discount applied to standard premium for workers compensation insurance and, in some states, automobile and general liability insurance when rated on a guaranteed cost basis. The amount of the discount is determined by using a table approved by insurance regulators. As the premium increases, so does the discount. Basically, the discount recognizes that the costs of writing and issuing an insurance policy do not rise in proportion to the premium once premiums reach a certain level (e.g., $1,000).

Products-completed operations aggregate: the maximum limit of liability payable by an insurer on behalf of an insured for all products and completed operations losses during any given annual policy period.

Products-completed operations liability: the liability for bodily injury or property damage incurred by a merchant or manufacturer as a consequence of some defect in a product sold or manufactured or the liability incurred by a contractor for bodily injury or property damage arising from a completed job. This coverage is provided by the standard commercial general liability policies unless excluded by endorsement.

Professional liability: the professional person's or the organization's liability for damages. The purpose of professional liability insurance is to protect this person or organization against liability for damages (and the cost of defense) based upon his or her alleged or real professional errors and omissions or mistakes. This is also called *errors and omissions* insurance. Some of the available forms include: architects/engineers, medical malpractice, attorneys, law enforcement officers, pharmacists, trust department, escrow agents, accountants, and veterinarians.

Pro rata cancellation: the cancellation of an insurance policy or bond with the return premium credit being the full proportion of premium for the unexpired term of the policy or bond. This is in contrast to short-rate cancellation where the return premium is less than the pro rata unearned premium.

Rate: in fire and marine insurance, the cost of a unit of insurance. In other words, the fire insurance rate is applied to the insured value. In casualty insurance, rate is the annual cost per unit of the insurance company's exposure to loss. In other words, a casualty insurance (e.g., workers compensation, general liability) rate is applied to an appropriate exposures base (e.g., payroll or sales).

Rating bureau: an organization that collects statistical data on losses and exposures of businesses and promulgates rates for use by insurers in calculating premiums. The two most important rating bureaus are the National Council on Compensation Insurance and the Insurance Services Office, Inc. However, a number of states also use their own rating bureaus.

Reinsurance: insurance in which one insurer, the reinsurer, accepts all or part of the exposures insured in a policy issued by another insurer, the ceding insurer. In essence, it is insurance for insurance companies. It allows insurers to spread the risks of one policy among themselves and thereby write limits higher than one company would feel comfortable doing alone. *Facultative reinsurance* involves a one-time reinsurance transfer arranged specifically on a single policy. *Treaty reinsurance* involves an agreement in which a certain amount of the exposures of all policies written by the ceding company are automatically reinsured; in return, the reinsurer receives a percentage of all the premiums on the reinsured book of business.

Retention plan: a rating plan normally used in writing workers compensation insurance. This plan provides that the net cost to the policyholder is equal to a "retention factor" (insurance company profit and expenses) plus actual incurred losses subject to a maximum premium equal to standard premium less premium discount. With a retention plan, the full guaranteed cost premium is paid to the insurer. At the end of the policy period, the calculation is made and the premium is adjusted. If a return premium is indicated, it is paid as dividends to the insured.

Retroactive date: a provision found in many claims-made policies. The policy will not cover claims for injuries or damages that occurred prior to the retroactive date even if the claim is first made during the policy period.

Retrospective rating: a rating plan that adjusts the premium, subject to a specified minimum and maximum, to reflect the current loss experience of the insured. Retrospective rating combines actual losses with graded expenses to produce a premium that more accurately reflects the loss experience of the insured. The adjustment, of course, is performed after the policy has expired.

Risk and Insurance Management Society (RIMS): a nonprofit association dedicated to the advancement of professional standards in risk management. Its membership consists of corporations, institutions, and governmental entities in the United States, Canada, and abroad. RIMS sponsors an annual educational conference and publishes educational materials for use by risk managers.

Risk management: the practice of analyzing all noncompetitive (nonproduction, pure risks) exposure to risk of loss (loss by fortuitous or accidental means) and taking steps to minimize those potential or real losses to levels acceptable to the organization. It provides a systematic process for treating pure risk: identification and analysis of exposures, selection of appropriate risk management techniques to handle exposures, implementation of chosen techniques, and monitoring of the results. Methods for treating pure risks include: retention, contractual or noninsurance transfer, loss control, avoidance, and insurance transfer. A risk manager is an employee whose duty it is to establish and administer a risk management program for his or her employers.

Risk Retention Act: federal legislation that facilitates the formation of purchasing groups and group self-insurance for commercial liability exposures.

Self-insurance: a formal system whereby a firm pays out of operating earnings or a special fund any losses that occur, losses that could ordinarily be covered under an insurance program. The moneys that would normally be used for premium payments may be added to this special fund for payment of losses incurred.

Self-insured retention: the amount of each loss for which the insured agrees to be responsible before an umbrella or excess liability insurer begins to participate in a loss. A policy's full limit of liability applies in excess of a true self-insured retention. This is in contrast to a deductible which is subtracted from the policy limit.

Short-rate cancellation: a term used in insurance and bonding to describe the charge required for insurance or bonds in place for less than 1 year. Also it denotes the penalty assessed on the return premium for insurance or bonds canceled by the insured before the end of the policy period or term of the bond. Insurance policies provide that returned premiums be subject to short-rate cancellation if the insured cancels, but a pro rata return is provided if the insurer cancels.

Specified perils coverage: an alternative to comprehensive coverage on automobiles that provides named perils rather than all risks physical damage insurance. The named perils typically include fire, theft, flood, earthquake, windstorm, vandalism and malicious mischief, hail, and explosion. This coverage is slightly less costly than comprehensive coverage.

Standard premium: the premium developed by multiplying the appropriate rate times the proper exposure unit. This figure is then modified by experience rating, if applicable. If the risk is not subject to experience rating, the premium at manual rate is the standard premium.

Subrogation: the assignment to an insurer by terms of the policy or by law, after payment of a loss, of the rights of the insured to recover the amount of the loss from one legally liable for it. After the insurer pays the insured's claim, it subrogates against the party that caused the loss to recover the amount paid. Business managers should make certain that subrogation recoveries from third parties are subtracted from loss data used in experience rating or retrospective rating calculations.

Supplemental extended reporting period: the optional extended reporting period (unlimited duration) under the 1986 ISO claims-made commercial general liability policy. The insured must request and pay for this coverage in order to activate it. It covers both known and unknown losses that occurred on or after the policy's retroactive date and on or before its expiration date.

Tax factor: an amount applied to an insurance premium to increase it to cover state premium taxes. This is one of the factors used in the retrospective rating formula.

Umbrella liability insurance: a form of excess liability insurance available to protect against claims in excess of the limits of other primary policies or for claims not covered by the primary insurance program. This latter coverage requires the insured to be a self-insurer for a specified amount ($10,000 to $25,000). It generally provides excess coverage over the insured's auto liability, commercial general liability, and employers liability policies. Care must be taken to coordinate all primary and excess policies to avoid coverage gaps.

Vendors single interest: insurance for financial institutions that protects against financial loss from physical damage to property (collateral) on which loans have been made in the event the borrower does not have physical damage coverage in place. It is most commonly used in conjunction with automobile, motorcycle, and mobile home loans. The insurance protects only the outstanding loan amount owed to the financial institution. Even though borrowers frequently pay the premium, they receive no insurance protection for their equity. This type of insurance is extremely expensive, and business managers should take all necessary steps to avoid having it purchased on financed property.

Workers compensation: compensation—required by laws in all states—to workers injured while on the job, whether or not the employer has been negligent. Benefits vary according to state laws but generally require the payment of medical expenses and partial wage continuation. The workers compensation laws apply to all individuals except those specifically excluded. Employers are required by law to purchase insurance for their exposure unless they file for and obtain permission to become qualified self-insurers.

Wrap-up insurance program: also called an *owner-controlled insurance program* (OCIP), this involves the purchase by a building project owner of workers compensation and liability insurance on behalf of all or most involved contractors. If properly designed and administered, this type of program can substantially reduce insurance costs as compared to what the contractors would otherwise collectively pay and pass on to the owner.

Index

About the Authors

WILLIAM S. MCINTYRE IV, has experienced a 24-year career as an insurance agent, an insurance/risk management consultant, and an underwriter. He is president of American Contractors Insurance Group and is a technical advisor for International Risk Management Institute's reference manuals and chairman of its annual Construction Insurance Conference. McIntyre speaks often at insurance industry meetings and is the author of many articles on insurance and risk management topics.

JACK P. GIBSON is president of International Risk Management Institute, Inc. (IRMI), which publishes newsletters and reference manuals for insurance buyers, agents, brokers, and underwriters. Prior to joining IRMI, he was a consultant with a leading international risk management firm. The author of numerous articles in his field, Gibson has been awarded Chartered Property Casualty Underwriter, Chartered Life Underwriter, and Associate in Risk Management designations.